EXPLORING THE NATURE AND GIFT OF DREAMS

EXPLORING THE NATURE AND GIFT OF DREAMS

How to Understand Your Dream Language

JAMES W. GOLL

DESTINY IMAGE® PUBLISHERS, INC.
P.O. Box 310, Shippensburg, PA 17257-0310

"Speaking to the Purposes of God for This Generation and for the Generations to Come."

This book and all other Destiny Image, Revival Press, MercyPlace, Fresh Bread, Destiny Image Fiction, and Treasure House books are available at Christian bookstores and distributors worldwide.

For a U.S. bookstore nearest you, call 1-800-722-6774.
For more information on foreign distributors, call 717-532-3040.
Reach us on the Internet: www.destinyimage.com.

This book was previously published by The Encounters Network as *Dream Language Study Guide,* by James W. and Michal Ann Goll.

ISBN 10: 0-7684-2752-5
ISBN 13: 978-0-7684-2752-3

For Worldwide Distribution, Printed in the U.S.A.

1 2 3 4 5 6 7 8 9 10 11 / 13 12 11 10 09

Dedication

With gratefulness, we dedicate this study guide to Jesus—our Dream Come True!

Endorsements

James Goll tells his story of discovering God's dream for his life. You will find help in this book to understand and follow God's directions in your own life.

Billy Joe Daugherty
Victory Christian Center, Tulsa, OK

James Goll is a superb writer and he has delivered marvelously on a very pertinent topic for these days. The Bible has much to say about dreams, and James helps put the whole topic into clear perspective for us.

Pat Williams
Senior Vice President, Orlando Magic

James and Michal Ann Goll have blessed us with vital truths and living examples to understand and fulfill dreams. The reader will discover the real purpose and meaning of dreams. Biblical and practical guidelines are given to help an individual discern whether the dream was divinely given and how to properly apply its meaning. James and Michal Ann, thanks for helping us to understand and fulfill our spiritual dreams.

Dr. Bill Hamon
Apostle, Bishop of Christian International Ministries Network

Francis Bacon said, "Reading maketh a full man speaking, a ready man; writing, an exact man." After reading James' book I would add…"and dreaming, a complete man." Those dreams I once dismissed now have meaning, and I have the prophetic guide, James Goll to thank. For God speaks in the language of image, symbol, color, and sense, and nobody does a better job of explaining the prophetic realm and its language than James Goll.

Dr. Lance Walnau
Lance Learning Group

Everyone is dreaming! It's just one of the languages of Heaven. If we are to interpret the signs and the times then we need master technicians to help us. It has been my great pleasure to know and work with James and Michal Ann Goll. I cannot think of anyone more spiritually prepared or experienced in the pragmatics of dream language than this couple. I have heard them teach on intrinsic and extrinsic dreams in particular…brilliant! That alone is worth the price of this book. If you're a dreamer, then interpreting dream language is a must. This is a book that will put wings under the feet of the process that you need to move quickly into that new land of the Spirit that awaits.

Graham Cooke

Table of Contents

Preface 13

Part One: Building the Framework **15**

Lesson One: The Master Dream Weaver 17

Lesson Two: My Personal Dream Journey 27

Lesson Three: Learning Your Spiritual Alphabet 37

Lesson Four: Creating a Culture for Revelation 43

Part Two: Learning the Vocabulary **55**

Lesson Five: Dreams Work! 57

Lesson Six: The Diversity of Dreams 67

Lesson Seven: Understanding the Dreams You Dream 77

Lesson Eight: Properly Interpreting Dreams 85

Part Three: Walking in Wisdom **97**

Lesson Nine: Stops Along the Way 99

Lesson Ten: Journaling as a Tool for Retaining Revelation 115

Lesson Eleven: When God Seems Silent 123

Lesson Twelve: Handling Dreams With Wisdom 133

Answers to the Reflection Questions 145

Recommended Reading 149

Index of Dream Symbols and Types 151

Instructional Guidelines and Reference Materials

The following study guide, *Exploring the Nature and Gift of Dreams*, has been prepared especially for you by James W. and Michal Ann Goll. The lessons are tailor-made with your individual, small group, or training center needs in mind. At the end of each lesson, there are Reflection Questions to help you in your review of the materials you have studied. In a back section of this study guide, you will find the answers to the Reflection Questions to aid in your learning.

Encounters Network also has available for purchase the CDs or DVDs that match up with each lesson. Use this study guide alone, or, for a more thorough understanding, order the corresponding CD/DVD messages from our Resource Center.

This study guide directly corresponds with the book *Dream Language* published by Destiny Image Publishers in 2006. The twelve lessons in this study guide also correspond with the following messages on CD or DVD:

Part One: Building the Framework

Lesson One: The Master Dream Weaver—CD 1/DVD 1

Lesson Two: My Personal Dream Journey—CD 2/DVD 2

Lesson Three: Learning Your Spiritual Alphabet—CD 3/DVD 2

Lesson Four: Creating a Culture for Revelation—CD 4/DVD 3

Part Two: Learning the Vocabulary

Lesson Five: Dreams Work! (by Michal Ann Goll)—CD 5/DVD 3

Lesson Six: The Diversity of Dreams—CD 6 & 7/DVD 4

Lesson Seven: Understanding the Dreams You Dream—CD 8/DVD 5

Lesson Eight: Properly Interpreting Dreams—CD 9/DVD 5

Part Three: Walking in Wisdom

Lesson Nine: Stops Along the Way (by Michal Ann Goll)—CD 10/DVD 6

Lesson Ten: Journaling as a Tool of Retaining Revelation—CD 11/DVD 6

Lesson Eleven: When God Seems Silent—CD 12/DVD 7

Lesson Twelve: Handling Dreams With Wisdom—CD 13/DVD 7

You may place orders for materials from Encounters Network's Resource Center on our Web site at www.encountersnetwork.com or by calling 1-877-200-1604. You may also mail your orders to P.O. Box 470470, Tulsa, OK, 74147-0470. An order sheet is enclosed at the back of this manual for your convenience. For more information, visit our Web site or send an e-mail to info@encountersnetwork.com.

If you have benefited from this study guide, James W. Goll has many other study guides available for purchase.

Preface

Most of us find ourselves drowning in busyness, never allowing ourselves to find the place of silence where we can pause to ponder the mysteries of God's design for our life. It is in those private places that God's presence and God's Word will invade our lives. It is there that God comes to us to reveal Himself in unique ways.

Through dreams, God communicates with us concerning our destiny, as well as the destinies of our families, our nation, and our world. Part One of this study guide will help you build the framework that will enable you to understand the work of God in your dream life.

One-third of your life is spent in the dream world, and while your body rests, your subconscious is actively involved in dreaming. In the dream world, the language is more spiritual and symbolic; if you are not learned in this heavenly dream language, then you will misinterpret the meaning. In Part Two, I will provide some instruments of interpretation that will help you understand dream language so that you can capture its full intended content.

In Part Three, I will focus on journaling, the silence of God, and learning to handle dreams with wisdom. When dealing with dreams, visions, and revelation, we will each surely need to know the wisdom ways of God.

Remember to use the Reflection Questions at the end of each lesson. They will help you to process what you are learning and put into practice what God is revealing to you. May God bless you as you go through this study, for He truly is the answer to all your dreams.

James W. Goll

PART 1

BUILDING
THE
FRAMEWORK

The Master Dream Weaver

I. Introduction

God is the Master Dream Weaver. Through dreams, God communicates directly with us concerning our destiny, as well as the destinies of our families, our nation, and our world. Many people today, particularly in the Western culture, never recognize God speaking to them in this way because they have been conditioned by a skeptical and sophisticated society to discount the language of dreams. Within our own generation, God is reconnecting us to a vital part of our spiritual heritage.

II. The Language of Heaven

Over 200 times the Scriptures give reference to dreams and visions. Three hundred times the Scriptures refer to angels. God is a supernatural God, and He communicates to His people through supernatural means.

A. **What Is a Dream?** A dream is a series of thoughts, images, or emotions that appear in our minds during sleep. Sometimes they are straightforward, but most of the time they are not. In the case of Holy Spirit-inspired dreams, often there is the need for careful interpretation, as these dreams tend to be parabolic in nature. In other words, like the parables of Jesus, the meaning of a dream is sometimes hidden.

B. **Mark 4:10-13:** *"As soon as He was alone, His followers, along with the twelve, began asking Him about the parables. And He was saying to them, 'To you has been given the mystery of the kingdom of God, but those who are outside get everything in parables, so that while seeing, they may see and not perceive, and while hearing, they may hear and not understand, otherwise they might return* *and be forgiven.' And He said to them, 'Do you not understand this parable? How will you understand all the parables?'"*

1. Jesus' pattern of teaching was to speak in parables and mysteries—not to keep people in the dark, but to <u>whet the appetite of those who were truly hungry for the truth.</u> He wanted to draw <u>them</u> in so they would press forward to know more. He loves this journey of hooking us with revelation with the purpose of actually reeling us into His very heart.

2. Dreams and visions often use parabolic language. Like parables, dreams are mysteries that need careful deciphering. Dream language is the mystical language of Heaven.

AMP: good (really)

C. **Mark 4:22-25:** *"'For nothing is hidden, except to be revealed; nor has anything been secret, but that it would come to light. If anyone has ears to hear, let him hear.' And He was saying to them, 'Take care what you listen to. By your standard of measure it will be measured to you; and more will be given you besides. For whoever has, to him more shall be given; and whoever does not have, even what he has shall be taken away from him.'"*

1. Things are hidden for a divine purpose: the purpose of being revealed. God is going to speak secrets to you—things that in the beginning you might not quite comprehend. But as you go on the journey and receive the spirit of wisdom and revelation, you will learn how to understand mysteries and secrets.

2. We need to be attentive. Listening in many ways is a lost art, but it's a vital skill we need to learn in order to become fluent in dream language.

III. Grounded in the Word

Walking in the fullness of the Spirit is like sailing. We must learn to put up the sail to catch the wind, so as to be driven along by it. That is like the moving of the Holy Spirit. We also need to have an anchor, which we can compare to the Word of God. At times we need to go into the harbor and drop the anchor, rest, meditate on the Word, and get refueled. But then there are other times you pick up your anchor (you carry the Word of God with you), put up the sail, catch the wind, and go where the Holy Spirit leads you. The anchor—the Word of God—is what grounds us, and what serves as a solid foundation.

A. **Numbers 12:6:** *"Hear now My words: If there is a prophet among you, I, the Lord, shall make Myself known to him in a vision. I shall speak with him in a dream."*

God says that He will speak to His people in a dream and that He will make Himself known in a vision. He uses both of these instruments to draw us into His purposes.

B. **Job 33:14-18:** *"Indeed God speaks once, or twice, yet no one notices it. In a dream, a vision of the night, when sound sleep falls on men, while they slumber in their beds, then He opens the ears of men, and seals their instruction, that He may turn man aside from his conduct, and keep man from pride; He keeps back his soul from the pit, and his life from passing over into Sheol."*

Our minds are often so preoccupied that it is hard for us to hear God. If He cannot catch our attention during our waking hours, He will speak to us during our sleep through dreams. Our heavenly Father will use dreams and visions as an avenue of identifying the hindrances that are in our path to His purpose.

C. **Joel 2:28-29:** *"It will come about after this that I will pour out My Spirit on all mankind; and your sons and daughters will prophesy, your old men will dream dreams, your young men will see visions. Even on the male and female servants I will pour out My Spirit in those days."*

Dreams and visions are a major part of the prophetic outpouring of God's great love in the last days!

D. **Hebrew Old Testament Words**

Three very similar Hebrew words are used in the Old Testament to refer to dreams. Whichever word is used, the Old Testament makes clear that God is the Master Dreamer. He downloads His dreams within us and thereby transforms us into dreamers as well.

1. *Chalam:* "to cause to dream" or "to be a dreamer"

2. *Chelem:* "to dream"

3. *Chalowm:* "dreamer"

E. Greek New Testament Words

1. *Onar:* the common word for "dream." It is the kind of dreaming we all do when we sleep. God can and does use these common dreams to communicate with ordinary people. Example: Joseph's dreams to wed Mary, escape to Egypt, and then return home, and the dreams of the wise men who were told not to return to Herod (see Matt. 1 and 2; also see Matt. 27:19).

2. *Enupnion:* refers to a vision or a dream received while asleep. *Enupnion* stresses a surprise quality that is contained in that dream. It is the kind of dream that has a startling effect, like waking suddenly from a dream and finding yourself strangely alert with your senses particularly acute. (Also see Jude, verse 8.)

IV. Historic Clips

Cessationism has done great damage in the Church. Cessationism is the basic teaching that the spiritual gifts stopped when the canon of Scriptures closed or when the last apostle passed away. The good news is that the Book of Hebrews says that Jesus Christ is the same yesterday, today, and forever (see Heb. 13:8). The truth is that the false doctrine of cessationism is going to cease because God's Word says, *"I'm going to pour out My Spirit upon all flesh"* (see Joel 2:28-29). What God did then, God does today, and God will continue to do. Dream language is the language of the ages. It is this mysterious way that God comes into our lives, invades our uncomfortable zones, and simply comes to speak to us.

A. Early Church Fathers

Great portions of the Church fathers' writings about dreams and visions have only recently been translated into English and have, therefore, been largely ignored in the past.

- Thomas of India received instruction from his dreams.

- Polycarp was given a vision of his martyrdom.

- Irenaeus had wise understanding of dreams.

- Clement believed that dreams come from the depth of the soul.

- Tertullian devoted eight chapters of his writings to dreams.

- Gregory of Nyssa spoke of the meaning and the place of the dream.

- John Chrysostom, the one who was called "golden mouthed" because he had such oratorical grace upon him, called dreams the source of revelation.

- Constantine was directed in a dream regarding the heavenly sign that he was to carry into battle.

- Thérèse de Lisieux changed her life because of a dream.

- John Newton, an early slave trader, was stopped in his tracks in his lifestyle and vocation by a dream from God. Newton's life was so turned around that he eventually became a chaplain to the king of England. He went on to write the hymn that is possibly one of the greatest Protestant hymns of all ages, "Amazing Grace."

B. Abraham Lincoln

It was said that Abraham Lincoln had a dream in which he saw his own body lying in state when he was President. I wonder what effect the dream had upon Abraham Lincoln and how it was used to help prepare him to be able to meet his Maker at any moment.

C. Rev. A.J. Gordon

The following is an amazing dream that impacted a man who became one of the great pulpiteers in America. The Gordon-Conwell Theological Seminary in Boston, Massachusetts, is named after him. The Rev. A.J. Gordon, a famous Baptist preacher of Boston, told of a dream that drastically changed his ministry, even though he had never paid attention to dreams before this.

"I was in the pulpit before a full congregation, just ready to begin my sermon, when a stranger entered and passed slowly up the aisle as though silently asking with his eyes if someone would give him a seat. Halfway up the aisle, a gentleman stepped out and offered him a place in his pew, which was quietly accepted. As I began my sermon, my attention became riveted on this hearer. I said constantly to myself, 'Who can that stranger be?' After the service ended, the visitor had left before I could reach him. The gentleman with whom he had sat remained behind, however. I asked him, 'Can you tell me who that stranger was who sat in your pew this morning?' In the most matter-of-course way he replied: 'Why, do you not know that man? It was Jesus of Nazareth.'"[1]

The dream was the seminal event out of which came a complete change in Gordon's approach to ministry and a vivid transformation in his parishioners. This dream is written in his book, *How Christ Came to Church: The Pastor's Dream.* A.J. Gordon never preached a sermon again to please men. He preached as though his guest was the Man Christ Jesus, and he preached to please Him.

V. The Receiver

The secret to becoming a good dreamer is to become a good receiver. God not only sends dreams to those who believe in Him, but also to unbelievers because He wants their hearts to turn to Him.

A. Dreams to Prophets

1. Abraham (see Gen. 15:12-17).

2. Jacob (see Gen. 28:12; 31:10).

3. Daniel (see Dan. 7).

B. Dreams to Unbelievers

1. Abimelech (see Gen. 20:3).

2. Laban (see Gen. 31:24).

3. Midian (see Judg. 7:13-14).

4. Pharaoh's butler and baker (see Gen. 40:5).

5. Pharaoh (see Gen. 41:7;15-24).

6. Nebuchadnezzar (see Dan. 2:1,4,36).

7. Wise men (see Matt. 2:12).

8. Pilate's wife (see Matt. 27:19).

C. Dreams to Other Believers

1. Solomon (see 1 Kings 3:5).

2. Joseph (see Matt. 1:20).

VI. The Transmitter

Every receiver needs a transmitter. In human experience, dream transmission originates from any one of three different sources:

A. Personal God (see Acts 17:26-28).

B. Natural Man (see Ezek. 13:1-6, Jer. 23:16).

C. Demonic Darkness (see Acts 16:16-18).

VII. The Purpose

Proverbs 25:2: *"It is the glory of God to conceal a matter, but the glory of kings is to search out a matter."*

It's the glory of a king to search something out. You're a king and God gives you the right to go into the King's palace. He wants to give you the keys of revelation to be able to search something out. Being able to understand revelation is about being a son, a daughter. It's about kingship. What are dreams for? To whet your appetite, because if you're left musing, you're more likely to find out what the dream was all about.

VIII. The Invitation

God has a dream for your life, and He wants you to have the spirit of revelation upon your life. He has a great plan, and He wants to use these ways to speak to you. Perhaps you will be a Joseph: you'll have a dream, blab it prematurely, get in all kinds of trouble, and end up learning about the ways of God—not just the knowledge of God. May God raise up such a people in the earth that the world will come and say, "Behold, here comes the dreamer."

We live for Christ, but we also live to release the fragrance of His presence wherever we go. I don't want to live an ordinary life; I want to live a supernatural life that would cause people to say, "Who is that strange man crying in the wilderness? Behold, here is a dreamer."

Closing Prayer: *Lord, I ask for Your grace, and that the Spirit of wisdom and revelation would be released to us. Dream through us and weave an incredible tapestry for the world to see. For Jesus' sake, amen.*

Endnote

1. A.J. Gordon, *How Christ Came to Church: the Pastor's Dream* (Philadelphia, PA: American Baptist Publishing Society., 1895), 63, quoted in Kelsey, God, Dreams, and Revelation, 163-164.

Reflection Questions
Lesson One: The Master Dream Weaver

Answers to these questions can be found in the back of the study guide.

1. We have been conditioned by a _____ and _____ society to discount the language of dreams. God wants to reconnect us to a vital part of our spiritual _____.

2. A dream is _____.

3. Jesus spoke in parables and mysteries, not to keep people in the dark, but to _____ the appetite of those who are truly _____ for the truth.

4. Our heavenly Father will use dreams and visions as an avenue of identifying the _____ that are in our path to His purpose.

5. Hebrews 13:8 says that Jesus Christ is the _____, yesterday, today, and forever. What God did in the Bible, God does _____, and God will continue to do.

6. The secret to becoming a good dreamer is to become a good _____.

7. List four unbelievers and four believers in the Bible to whom God spoke through dreams.

   _____   _____

   _____   _____

   _____   _____

   _____   _____

8. List the three sources of dream transmission:

   _____ _____ _____

9. Write down below a recent dream you had. Reflect upon its source and whether it was parabolic in nature. Ask the Master Dream Weaver to speak to you through dreams and release the spirit of revelation upon your life.

My Personal Dream Journey

I. Dark Beginnings

The beginnings of my dream history were dark beginnings. My dreams were both dark from their source and dark in their content. A man would come in those dreams and taunt me. At times I would wake up out of the dreams and be catapulted to an open vision. The man would stand at the end of my bed, raise up a butcher knife, and was ready to bring it down. Somehow the vision or the dream would break up, and I would wake up to a room saturated with the presence of terror. It was actually a spirit of death.

My mother had a miscarriage of a little boy on July 3, 1951. That day she prayed to the Lord and said, "Lord, if you will give me another son, I will dedicate him to Christ's service." I was born exactly one year later on that very day, July 3rd, 1952, but I was also born with the cord wrapped around my neck. Because of this, I was born with a blue head. Blue is the color of revelation. So although the enemy meant harm for me, God turned this for good as I wanted to have the spirit of revelation.

II. Points of Reference

I had three prayers growing up. The inspiration for these prayers was supernatural because I don't believe a kid can come up with these. I prayed these prayers when I was young and throughout my teenage years. I continue praying them to this day:

1. "God, I ask that You would raise up Your Joseph counselors to those in authority, just as You did in days gone by."

I grew up in Missouri, and I became a personal intercessor for a man who became a U.S. senator from Missouri, then became the governor, and eventually the Attorney General of the United States. He retired in 2005—Attorney General John Ashcroft. The Lord use to show me about this righteous man in dreams and visions, that the hand of God would rest upon him, and that he would have the spirit of Joseph upon his life. God called me as a young guy to pray for a man named John Ashcroft, that he would be raised with the spirit of wisdom as a Joseph counselor to those in authority. Sure enough, it came to pass.

2.   "Lord, like Solomon, give me wisdom beyond my years."

As I get older I'm praying, "Lord, I need some more." I encourage you to pray those prayers, such as, "God, give me the spirit of counsel. Lord, give me a spirit of wisdom that goes beyond my years, beyond my natural training and knowledge."

3.   "God, give me a heart of purity that will keep me from the evil way."

These are keys to unlocking the spirit of revelation upon your life or upon anyone's life.

III. Immersed in the Spirit

In 1972, I went to a strange event at the Cotton Bowl in Dallas, Texas. It was one of the very early Jesus People gatherings. I ran into these weird people. They looked different than I did and dressed differently, but they were so on fire for God and witnessed to me about things like speaking in tongues, prophecy, deliverance, and the baptism in the Holy Spirit. I was a Methodist, so I really didn't understand what they were talking about, but I sure liked their fervency.

Eventually the Holy Spirit twisted my arm hard enough, and I prayed something like, "God gives that to those who need it, and I don't need it." Eventually God convinced me that He does indeed give to those who need it, and I needed anything and everything He had! I became filled with the Holy Spirit with the release of His gifts, which included visions and praying and worshiping in the gift of tongues. These became an absolute lifeline for me.

Before being filled with the Holy Spirit, my life was like watching a small black and white TV set. Overnight it shifted to "omni-vision." I would see pictures, or have dreams and visions in full, vivid color. As I would walk on campus, I would see a person that I'd seen in a dream or vision the day or week before. I didn't know them, and I would go up to them and share with them what God had given to me. It worked! Dreams and visions are amazing, and they will unlock purposes of God for you. They will unlock dimensions of life for you that will take the mundane and make it extraordinary.

IV. The Master's Degree

In the late 1980s, I was ministering in northern Germany and had a dream. In this dream a seer prophet named John Paul Jackson, who stood two to three times his normal size, pointed his finger at me and said, "You will receive the Master's Degree as a Communication Specialist and as an Interpreter of Speech."

When I woke up, the riveting presence of God was all over me, and I was immediately catapulted into an open vision where I saw a man bent over in a field, hoeing. The man straightened up, looked at me, and said, "You will be the answer to our prayers." I didn't understand that at all. Even though I was in Germany, the Goll family's ancestral homeland, I knew of no righteous generational history. I was the first American Goll to return to German soil.

I continued my trip ministering in several eastern European countries. I preached with everything I had because I thought it might be the last time I was ever going to preach. I took the words of my dream and believed them literally. I began to anticipate going back to college for a Master's Degree in speech communication or another related field. I did not realize that dreams are more like mysteries or parables.

When I got back home, I was asked to teach on the subject of prophetic intercession at one of the big Passion for Jesus conferences in Kansas City, Missouri. The Lord had spoken to me, "Preach as though it's the last time you're ever going to preach." Four thousand people attended the workshop; it was an absolutely amazing event. God's presence was released powerfully, and the burden of the Lord gripped people's hearts.

I thought I was headed off to college, but the Lord showed me that my interpretation was incorrect. The Lord was saying to me, "I want to give you something you cannot earn and that you cannot learn at school. I want to give you My Master's Degree." I don't know how far along in that journey I am right now, but I am in a passionate pursuit, not only for the spirit of revelation, but also the grace to interpret that revelation and make clear the signs and wonders of speech.

V. Word Grafting

My personal dream journey has also involved "grafting" the Word of God into my being. The word grafting comes from the terminology in James 1:21: *"Therefore, putting aside all filthiness and all that remains of wickedness, in humility, receive the word implanted, which is able to save your souls."* When you implant or engraft the Word into your soul, your mind, your will, and your emotions, the Word is able to change you and save you.

A. **John 5:19-20:** *"Therefore Jesus answered and was saying to them, 'Truly, truly, I say to you, the Son can do nothing of Himself, unless it is something He sees the Father doing; for whatever the Father does, these things the Son also does in like manner. For the Father loves the Son, and shows Him all things that He Himself is doing; and the Father will show Him greater works than these, so that you will marvel.'"*

Even as the Son could do nothing apart from the Father, so it should be with us. Our prayer should be, "Father, show us what You are doing so that we can model it in the earth."

B. **Romans 6:13-16:** *"Do not go on presenting the members of your body to sin as instruments of unrighteousness; but present yourselves to God as those alive from the dead, and your members as instruments of righteousness to God. For sin shall not be master over you, for you are not under law but under grace. What then? Shall we sin because we are not under law but under grace? May it never be! Do you not know that when you present yourselves to someone as slaves for obedience, you are slaves of the one whom you obey, either of sin resulting in death, or of obedience resulting in righteousness?"*

If you want to mature in the spirit of revelation, surrender every member of your being to be mastered by the Lord Jesus Christ.

C. **Ephesians 1:17-19:** *"...that the God of our Lord Jesus Christ, the Father of glory, may give to you a spirit of wisdom and of revelation in the knowledge of*

Him. I pray that the eyes of your heart may be enlightened, so that you will know what is the hope of His calling, what are the riches of the glory of His inheritance in the saints, and what is the surpassing greatness of His power toward us who believe. These are in accordance with the working of the strength of His might."

I have probably prayed these verses ten times a day for over ten years. Ask the Lord, "Open the eyes of my heart, Lord, that I might see You and know Your ways."

D. **2 Kings 6:17:** *"Then Elisha prayed and said, 'O Lord, I pray, open his eyes that he may see.' And the Lord opened the servant's eyes and he saw; and behold, the mountain was full of horses and chariots of fire all around Elisha."*

In the beginning, I was not a seer; I was a hearer. I was a feeler, but I did not see. I would graft this verse within my being and pray that my spiritual eyes would be opened so that I could see into the revelatory realm. You can ask the Lord for this as well.

E. **Genesis 40:8:** *"Then they said to him, 'We have had a dream and there is no one to interpret it.' Then Joseph said to them, 'Do not interpretations belong to God? Tell it to me, please.'"*

Joseph understood that dreams came from the Lord and their interpretations did also. Don't just pray for the spirit of revelation; pray also for the ability to interpret. The same God who gave the revelation is able to give you the interpretation.

VI. A Wife Who Soars

On October 4, 1992—the Day of Atonement—my sweet, compliant wife received a divine visitation that transformed her life and mine. A lightning bolt struck near the back of our house, and the light of it flashed through our bedroom window. A man (an angel) stood in our bedroom, looked at me for one minute and said, "Watch your wife. I'm about to speak to her." The angel departed, and my wife woke up. I said to her, "Ann, an angel has just come." We pulled the covers over our heads and shook for about a half an hour. Then I miraculously fell asleep.

Michal Ann was then caught up in the spirit realm and had a dramatic encounter with the Lord. She actually got up and went into the bathroom to look at herself because she thought the force of the encounter had rearranged her bones and turned her hair white.

Our lives catapulted into a new dimension. I would be out traveling, going on the road to speak different places, and I would call home to find out what God was saying. I did not previously believe that women belonged in ministry, let alone in leadership, but God rearranged our lives radically. I remember standing in the kitchen one night looking at my wife and saying, "I don't know who you are or who you're becoming." She looked at me and said, "That's good because I don't know who I am or who I'm becoming, either." Michal Ann's visitations literally went on for nine weeks.

Before all this had happened, my wife had cried out to the Lord, "Oh God, I just want to be with You, I just want to spend time with You, I just want to hear You." We had four little children, we were building a house, and I was traveling frequently. God spoke to her and said, "I know you don't have much time, but I am going to come to you in the night seasons, and I will speak to you in dreams."

We believe that what the Lord did for Michal Ann is a parable for the Body of Christ. God is coming to awaken His Bride, to release dreams and visions, angelic visitations, signs, and wonders, so that the one who has been timid is changed by His presence.[1]

VII. Guided in the Night

Spiritual dreams are your inheritance. These dreams generally fall into three categories:

1. God speaking to your spirit
2. Your spirit crying out to God
3. God's Spirit interceding through your spirit

Like Michal Ann, I have had many experiences of being guided by dreams in the night. I have received dreams of a personal nature, dreams about the Church, dreams about cities, dreams about nations, dreams about wars, and dreams calling me to intercede so that wars will stop.

In August of 2003, I had a dream in which I saw a huge army coming up to me. I was afraid that they were going to overwhelm me completely. Then, suddenly, the whole perspective of my dream changed. As they approached, I began to grow until I was two or three times my normal stature. I was looking down on my enemies. As I looked at this change, the word of the Lord came on the wind and said, "And your enemies shall become like grasshoppers in your own sight."

When I woke up I thought the dream was imparting a message for me to teach others—and it may have been. However, about three weeks later I found a suspicious lump under my skin, which quickly grew to the size of a cluster of grapes. I was diagnosed with non-Hodgkin's lymphoma, a cancer. I thought back to my dream of a few weeks before. Little had I "dreamed" at the time that I would be the one who needed the message of that dream! Yet *God* knew.

We shared this dream with those we walked with and with our prayer partners. I asked them, "Help me keep my feet to that dream that my enemies—the enemies of my soul—will become like grasshoppers in my own sight." We prayed my dream, and I still stand today on God's promise that came to me in that amazing dream.

Closing Prayer: *Impart to us an awakened spirit. Come and speak to us secrets and the kind of dream language encounter where faith will be released into each one of us and spiritual courage will be stirred up. In the name of Jesus, enroll each one of us in the school of the Holy Spirit, that we would all receive the Master Jesus certificate of graduation, the Master's Degree in dream language, in Jesus' great name. Amen.*

Endnote

1. For a fuller account of Michal Ann's experience, refer to our book *God Encounters* (Shippensburg, PA: Destiny Image Publishers, Inc., 2005) and Michal Ann's book *Women on the Front Line* (Shippensburg, PA: Destiny Image Publishers, Inc. 1998).

Reflection Questions
Lesson Two: My Personal Dream Journey

Answers to these questions can be found in the back of the study guide.

1. From Section II, review the three prayers I have prayed since I was a young child. If key prayers and/or Scriptures have been a part of your life, write them out below. If you do not have any, consider "adopting" one of mine, or ask the Lord to give you one.

2. Whether or not you have received the baptism of the Holy Spirit, ask the Holy Spirit to fill you, release His gifts to you, and unlock new dimensions of life in the Spirit for you. Write below one of the gifts of the Holy Spirit you desire the most and ask the Lord for it (see 1 Cor. 12:7-11; 14:13).

3. Think about any "Master's Degree program" that God has had you in. Write the name of that program below and the major "courses" that the Lord has led you through. Reaffirm in prayer right now your desire to remain in the school of the Holy Spirit.

4. From Section V, list below the five Scriptures that the Lord led me to graft into my mind, will, and emotions. Circle one the Holy Spirit is leading you to begin to graft into your being, or in the extra blank provided, write another Scripture the Holy Spirit leads you to implant into your mind, will, and emotions.

    _____   _____

    _____   _____

    _____   _____

5. If you are married or plan to be married, pray for your spouse (or future spouse, even if you do not know him/her) right now. Ask God to visit him/her powerfully, causing him/her to soar and be equally yoked with you spiritually.

6. Pause right now and ask the Lord to guide you in the night seasons—starting tonight!

LESSON THREE

Learning Your Spiritual Alphabet

I. The People Who Appear in My Dreams

In the majority of cases, the people who appear in your dreams are symbolic in nature. There are three main ways of interpreting these dreams:

1. Who is this person in relation to you?

2. What does the person's name mean?

3. What character trait or calling do they represent to you?

A. Tips for Understanding the People Who Appear in Your Dreams:

1. A man or woman of God in your life would most probably represent a message being delivered.

2. An untrustworthy person in your past could indicate a coming situation that should not be trusted.

3. A healing evangelist (prophetic person, etc.) represents a healing grace coming your way.

4. A husband in dreams often represents Christ Jesus drawing ever so near to you.

5. Getting married in dreams typically speaks of growing intimacy with God.

6. Dreams with dead people in them speak of the common sentiment attached to those deceased loved ones. These are *not* indications that

you are "crossing over" and actually visiting the person from the past to receive guidance.

7. Dreams of presidents and people in authority are often calls to pray for national events.

8. A faceless man often appears in dreams and is an indication of the Holy Spirit or possibly even angels in one's life.

II. R-Rated Dreams—Am I Sick or What?

A. Various Schools of Thought on Dreams of Sexual Content

These understandings take the following forms:

1. A spiritual call to greater intimacy

2. A warning of the need to cleanse attitudes of the mind, motives of the heart, and/or repent for acts of immorality

3. A calling or joining of union with another person or people group

4. Natural body dreams containing the biological and physical desires that are common to most people

B. Sexual Encounters

To understand these dreams properly consider the following questions:

1. Is it the same sex? Is it the opposite sex? (Much of the church world breeds only after their kind—but multiplication comes from sowing your seed into those who are opposite of you.)

2. Is it an old love or new one? (This could indicate what you are currently passionate about.)

3. Does this person seem to take the place of the Lord?

4. Does this dream leave you feeling dirty or clean?

5. Are you and or the others naked in a dream? (Transparency is a good thing. But often in these dreams everyone can see what is going on in your life. These dreams are not to embarrass you but to encourage you in your vulnerability with others.)

C. Various Quotations

1. From *Dreams and Visions* by Dr. Joe Ibojie

"Sex in a dream suggests that you are probably making, or about to make, decisions based on a carnal nature. In Scripture, God frequently uses sexual immorality as an allegory for unfaithfulness, or deviation from spiritual truth. Frequent experience of sex in dreams speaks of carnality, but it also indicates a hidden, unbroken stronghold of lust. Rape indicates violation of the dreamer's person or integrity, and this must be averted in prayer."[1]

2. From *Parables in the Night Season* by Joy Parrott

"God is not a prude, and He may give you some dreams that will have you sure they couldn't be from Him, yet they are. Of course, many of these will not be divine, especially if we continue to walk in the things of this world and satisfy our fleshly desires. Yet God has recorded some risqué things in the Scripture which confirms that He is not a prude. In the Book of Ezekiel, God refers to Jerusalem, His people, as harlots! In Hosea, God tells the prophet Hosea to marry a prostitute as a prophetic drama of His unconditional love for His people. God told Isaiah to run around naked for three years prophesying to everything in sight! Such examples show that God isn't concerned about offending us or sparing our 'holy ears' from hearing such things. He is going to speak in a language that we will understand."[2]

III. Learning Your Spiritual Alphabet

A. From *Dream* by Mark Rutland

"Believers must, of course, be cautious when seeking to understand dreams and even more prudent when acting on them. There is no substitute for wisdom and discernment in dream interpretation, and prayer is crucial to developing them. Believers should commit their subconscious minds to the Lord as well as their waking thoughts, and then seek from God, in earnest prayer, understanding for the visions of the night."[3]

B. **What Language Do You Speak?**

1 Corinthians 13:1: *"If I speak with the tongues of men and of angels…"*

We each have a personal walk and, in a sense, a personal talk. Your spiritual alphabet, though similar to someone else's, is unique. Journaling is a tool that will be used to capture your distinct pictures, grant understanding over time, and give wisdom for the journey. The Holy Spirit will guide you into truth; keep things safe, yet adventurous; pure, yet unreligious.

C. **Three Methods of Interpreting**

1. Use the **dictionary and Bible** to interpret words and symbols. Find the meaning in previous recordings of literature. See Kevin Conner's book *Interpreting Symbols and Types*. This is the best beginning way to interpret.

2. Through **journaling**, learn about your own dreams and grow in your personal spiritual alphabet. We each have a language and a unique vocabulary. Whatever your language is, the Holy Spirit will speak to you in that language.

3. By the **anointing, gifts, and presence of the Holy Spirit.**

D. **Closing Thought to Help Us Understand the Nature of Dreams**

"Dreams do not explain the future—the future will explain the dreams."

Endnotes

1. Joe Ibojie, *Dreams and Visions: How to Receive, Interpret, and Apply Your Dreams* (Pescara, Italy: Destiny Image Europe, 2005), 160.

2. Joy Parrott, *Parables in the Night Seasons: Understanding Your Dreams* (Renton, WA: Glory Publications, Joy Parrott Ministries, 2002), 57-58.

3. Mark Rutland, *Dream: Awake or Asleep, Unlock the Power of God's Vision* (Lake Mary, FL: Charisma House, 2003), 8-9.

Reflection Questions
Lesson Three: Learning Your Spiritual Alphabet

Answers to these questions can be found in the back of the study guide.

1. What are three good questions to ask yourself in order to understand people who appear in your dreams?

   1) _____

   2) _____

   3) _____

2. Review the eight tips to understanding the people who appear in your dreams. Record below a dream that you remember about a specific person and any increased insight about whom or what that person may represent.

3. If you have had any "R-rated" dreams, review Section II, especially the questions listed there to understand these dreams properly. Write below any point that helps you to understand more clearly dreams of this nature that you have had in the past.

4. "There is no substitute for _____ and _____ in dream interpretation, and _____ is crucial to developing them."

5. What are three methods of interpreting your spiritual alphabet?

   1) _____

   2) _____

   3) _____

6. Write below two main insights you gained from this lesson. Then spend a short time in prayer around those two points, asking the Lord to implant those messages in your heart.

7. If you have a personal alphabet with the Lord, write out below any consistent images (people, places, things) that God uses and what they represent to you. If you have recurring images and do not understand what they mean, ask the Lord right now for understanding and revelatory insight so you can begin to develop your own personal alphabet. Write out below anything the Lord shows to you.

Creating a Culture for Revelation

I. **Dream Snatchers**

There are many reasons why dreams appear to be lost after they have been caught. Let's keep things simple and clear. We have an enemy waiting to snatch away and steal the revelation that the Holy Spirit brings.

A. **The Thief Comes**

1. **Matthew 24:43:** *"But be sure of this, that if the head of the house had known at what time of the night the **thief** was coming, he would have been on the alert and would not have allowed his house to be broken into"* (emphasis added).

2. **Luke 12:39:** *"But be sure of this, that if the head of the house had known at what hour the **thief** was coming, he would not have allowed his house to be broken into"* (emphasis added).

3. **John 10:1:** *"Truly, truly, I say to you, he who does not enter by the door into the fold of the sheep, but climbs up some other way, he is a **thief** and a robber"* (emphasis added).

4. **John 10:10:** *"The **thief** comes only to steal and kill and destroy; I came that they may have life, and have it abundantly"* (emphasis added).

We must realize that throughout the ages the devil and the powers of darkness have made an assault against believers in an attempt to snuff out the gifts of the Spirit and the revelatory realms of God. The thief has been at work to steal the true power of the Holy Spirit and to raise a counterpart move under the influence of the occult. But Jesus will always prevail through His people, and the thief shall be identified, caught and be made to repay!

B.   The Thief Must and Can Be Caught

Proverbs 6:31: *"But when he* [the thief] *is found, he must repay sevenfold; he must give all the substance of his house."*

It is time to move into a higher dimension of the gifting of discerning of spirits and thus identify and capture the thief. Then we must enter into judicial intercession in a courtroom hearing and call forth retribution where judgment is released and justice occurs.

C.   The Thief Must Flee

James 4:7: *"Submit therefore to God. Resist the devil and he will flee from you"* (emphasis added).

Three simple components from James 4:7:

1.   Submit to God.

2.   Resist the devil.

3.   He runs in terror from you!

II.   The Drain to Dreaming

A.   Church Culture and Worldview

Wrong traditions, theology, and worldview have stolen the relevance of dreaming. We have erred by moving away from our Hebraic foundation and shifting into a Greek mindset. There is literally no place for dreams in a materialistic and logical scientism that has almost completely replaced the original paradigm of apostolic Christianity.

This philosophy produces the analytical mindset of "then why pay attention to them at all?"

B.   Are You at Rest or Are You Striving?

Ecclesiastes 4:6: *"One hand full of rest is better than two fists full of labor and striving after wind."*

Isaiah 30:15: *"For thus the Lord God, the Holy One of Israel, has said, 'In repentance and rest you will be saved, in quietness and trust is your strength....'"*

Rest is the incubation bed of revelation!

C. **Is Your Receptor Clean?**

Ephesians 4:23-27: *"Be renewed in the spirit of your mind, and put on the new self, which in the likeness of God has been created in righteousness and holiness of the truth. Therefore, laying aside falsehood, speak truth each one of you with his neighbor, for we are members of one another. Be angry, and yet do not sin; do not let the sun go down on your anger, and do not give the devil an opportunity."*

1.   Worry (see Ps. 37:8).

2.   Anger (see Eph. 4:26).

3.   Lust (see Rom. 13:13-14).

4.   Excess and addictions (see Eph. 5:18).

5.   Bitterness (see Heb. 12:15).

Our spirit must be able to receive. We must not give place to the devil. We must not grieve the Holy Spirit!

D. **Wisdom Ways With Today's Entertainment**

We must be careful what we listen to. What we let in our eyes and ears will be what our heart and mind will dwell on. We need a pure life revolution! Consider going on an entertainment fast!

Mark 4:24: *"And He was saying to them, 'Take care what you listen to. By your standard of measure it will be measured to you; and more will be given you besides.'"*

E. **Working With Your Routine!**

Inconsistent schedules can hinder the flow and retention of revelation. Often this is not our fault but simply due to the demands of life. Cry out to the Lord for God's grace, and He will help you to work with your schedule and/or even alter it as needed.

Seek the Lord for special times that are set apart for receiving from Him. Sacrifice releases power. Fasting can be used to soften your heart and position you for heavenly downloads.

F. To Whom Is Given Much?

Matthew 13:12-16: *"For whoever has, to him more shall be given, and he will have an abundance; but whoever does not have, even what he has shall be taken away from him. Therefore I speak to them in parables; because while seeing they do not see, and while hearing they do not hear, nor do they understand. In their case the prophecy of Isaiah is being fulfilled, which says, 'You will keep on hearing, but will not understand; you will keep on seeing, but will not perceive; for the heart of this people has become dull, with their ears they scarcely hear, and they have closed their eyes, otherwise they would see with their eyes, hear with their ears, and understand with their heart and return, and I would heal them.' But blessed are your eyes, because they see; and your ears, because they hear."*

If we do not pay attention to what we have already received, the Holy Spirit is not obligated to give us more—*"whoever has, to him more shall be given."*

Faithfulness brings reward!

G. Integrity Is a Major Issue!

Both the Holy Spirit and people are drawn to integrity. Tomorrow's call does not give you authority today! There is a learning process of being called, trained, and commissioned (and often retrained and recommissioned).

Don't distort the meaning of a dream out of your insecurity. Don't say more than God says or more than God said to say! Don't add "hamburger helper" and thus exceed your level of credibility. Learn to pray and hold—do not cheat—and watch how you say it! God always ultimately has to judge pride!

III. Dream Busters[1]

A. Distraction

If you are having a phone conversation with someone while trying to do three other things, chances are you won't absorb all that was intended in that call. There are many good things to do. But if we want to receive and retain revelation, then we will have to weed the garden of "distractions." This is one of the primary reasons why we are exhorted by Scripture to set our minds on things above and not on things of this earth. If we can capture the little foxes that spoil the vine, we will be amazed at all that God has to speak to us!

B. Disinformation

What does God have to say in His Word? Does God still speak today? Or has the false teaching of cessationism distorted your view? Too often, as Christians, we are looking to institutions, denominations, and uninformed people to provide our theology rather than basing it on the Word of God. This is why many people do not believe God speaks to them today—not because of anything the Bible actually says—but what others wrongly say it says! Remember, **Hosea 4:6** states, *"My people are destroyed for **lack of knowledge**. Because you have rejected knowledge, I also will reject you from being My priest. Since you have forgotten the law of your God, I also will forget your children"* (emphasis added).

Wrong information and lack of information produce a breeding ground for doubt.

C. Disbelief

Many cannot and will not hear the voice of the Holy Spirit in their lives because they simply do not believe God wants to speak to them! Disbelief can filter out God's love, care, revelation, and, at times, His empowerment.

We must remember that we serve an all-powerful, all-knowing God who has spoken, is speaking, and will continue to speak to His people. If we have fallen into unbelief, then our first step is to cry out, *"I do believe; help my unbelief."* (Mark 9:24).

D. The Downward Spiral

Satan always will attempt to thwart God's plans. Such was the case with the Israelites. When they were coming out of Babylon, they received a revelation from the Lord (see Jer. 29:10). The Israelites knew God's will for them was to return and rebuild the destroyed temple of the Lord. They had heard clearly from God! As the people gave in to the enemy's schemes, three things began to happen:

1. They fell into discouragement.

2. They fell into disillusionment.

3. They fell into disinterest.

This progression of events is often a pattern for what can happen in our lives. It takes an act of our own will to choose God's plan for possessing our inheritance. You can reverse the trend and end the downward spiral!

IV. Dream Catchers—Create Your Culture!

A. Pulling Out Your Spiritual Antenna

Just as you have to pull out your antenna in order to receive sound transmissions, you have to pull out your spiritual antenna to tune in and receive God's transmissions!

Get Ready! Expect to Receive!

The great British preacher Charles Spurgeon once received an entire sermon in a dream. He preached it aloud, and his wife, who was awake, copied it down. Later he preached the message from the pulpit to great effect.

Get Ready! Expect to Receive!

B. The Power of the Blood

Hebrews 9:12: *"...and not through the blood of goats and calves, but through His own blood, He entered the holy place once for all, having obtained eternal redemption."*

C. Pray in the Spirit

Build yourself up in your faith by praying in the Holy Spirit (see Jude 20). This is an amazing and underutilized gift! God promises to give us refreshment, stirring of our faith, and an atmosphere where mysteries are spoken and revealed. Get yourself ready! Strengthen your spirit man!

D. Meditation on the Word!

Joshua 1:8: *"This book of the law shall not depart from your mouth, but you shall meditate on it day and night, so that you may be careful to do according to* *all that is written in it; for then you will make your way prosperous, and then you will have success."*

E. **Worship—Sing Praises—Worship**

2 Chronicles 20:18-22: *"Jehoshaphat bowed his head with his face to the ground, and all Judah and the inhabitants of Jerusalem fell down before the Lord, worshiping the Lord. The Levites, from the sons of the Kohathites and of the sons of the Korahites, stood up to praise the Lord God of Israel, with a very loud voice. They rose early in the morning and went out to the wilderness of Tekoa; and when they went out, Jehoshaphat stood and said, 'Listen to me, O Judah and inhabitants of Jerusalem, put your trust in the Lord your God and you will be established. Put your trust in His prophets and succeed.' When he had consulted with the people, he appointed those who sang to the Lord and those who praised Him in holy attire, as they went out before the army and said, 'Give thanks to the Lord, for His lovingkindness is everlasting.' When they began singing and praising, the Lord set ambushes against the sons of Ammon, Moab and Mount Seir, who had come against Judah; so they were routed."*

V. **Our Hebraic Inheritance**

A. **Jewish Dream Practices**

The Traditional Jewish Bedtime Ritual

1. Dream Book—*sefer chalomot*

2. Reflection—*cheshbon hanefesh*

3. Bedtime Prayer—*Kriyat Sh'ma al hamita*

    a. One Who Casts Prayer—*Ha'mapil*

    b. Allegiance—*Sh'ma*

    c. Angel's Prayer—*Shekhinah*

    d. Sacred Intention—*Kavannah*

B. **Knowledge vs. Experience**

It is time for the Body of Christ to return to her Hebraic roots and expect to receive even in her sleep. Let's make the shift from the Greek over-emphasis on the mind and return to a heart-to-heart—spirit-to-spirit—encounter with a Living God!

May you have sweet heavenly sleep!

Endnote

1. Information in this section is adapted from Chuck D. Pierce and Rebecca Wagner Sytsema, *When God Speaks: How to Interpret Dreams, Visions, Signs and Wonders* (Ventura, CA: Gospel Light, 2005), 63-65.

Reflection Questions
Lesson Four: Creating a Culture for Revelation

Answers to these questions can be found in the back of the study guide.

1. We have an _____ waiting to _____ away and steal the _____ that the Holy Spirit brings.

2. According to James 4:7, when we _____ to God and _____ the devil, the devil will _____.

3. Wrong _____, _____, and _____ have stolen the relevance of dreaming. We have erred and moved away from our _____ foundation and shifted into a _____ mindset.

4. The Holy Spirit and people both are drawn to _____. Tomorrow's _____ does not give you _____ today!

5. List four dream busters. Circle the one that has primarily busted you in the past. Pause right now and ask God to bring breakthrough in this area.

    _____   _____

    _____   _____

6. List five dream catchers. Circle the one you believe the Lord wants you to focus on at this time. Pause right now and ask Him to help you lay hold of that area.

    _____   _____

    _____   _____

    _____

7. Matthew 13:12 says: *"For whoever has, to him more shall be given, and he will have an abundance; but whoever does not have, even what he has shall be taken away from him."* Write down a few of the main things God has entrusted to you. Pause and ask the Lord to help you to demonstrate faithfulness in these areas.

8. Write down the primary insight you gained from this lesson and how God is leading you to apply it to your life.

PART 2

LEARNING
THE
VOCABULARY

LESSON FIVE

Dreams Work!

By Michal Ann Goll

I. Life Impact

There were two pivotal points in time when the Lord changed my life through the supernatural activity of dreams. The first major point of impact dealt with healing my fractured perception of God my Father in relation to myself. The second impartation took me to a much deeper place beyond my needs and perceptions to see His aching heart for His Bride.

Being a wife and mother is an awesome privilege, but it also brings with it long days and short nights filled with constant busyness and responsibility. At the same time, I was longing for my spiritual walk with God to deepen and grow. God took my situation and breathed His creative swirl of release upon me. He changed me from a longing, hurting (but at the same time faithful and loyal) housewife and mother of four small children, to a Holy Spirit-charged woman of vision and power, secure and whole.

Do dreams really *work?* Will God really speak to *you* in your dreams? Can you really walk in the realm of dream language and revelation?" My answer to you is, "Yes!"

A. Childhood—Tornadoes and Bears

I was an active dreamer as a child, but unfortunately, many of my dreams were nightmares. My childhood nightmares seemed generally to center around two themes: tornadoes and bears.

1. **Generational Ties**

   Later in life my mother told me that she also had dreams of tornadoes. There were four children in our family, and she often dreamed that three of us were safe in the shelter with her while one child was outside somewhere. As the tornado approached, she would go outside and search for the missing child.

   Also, one Christmas my nephew, who was three years old at the time, was asleep in my *old bedroom*. In the middle of the night he woke up screaming, "The wind is going to get me! The wind is going to get me!" I believe there was a place of vulnerability that allowed entrance for those types of dreams. We had to come before the Lord, plead the blood of Jesus, and cut off the spirit of fear attached to those dreams.

2. **Redemptive View**

   - Tornadoes

   - Tornados can also symbolize the violent activity of God when He comes and shakes everything up. He rips out and demolishes the old dead stuff because He wants to bring in the new and impart life. God wants to shake up our understanding of what Christianity is supposed to look like. Sometimes God decides it is time to clean house.

   - Bears

   - Jim and I have always carried a burden in our hearts for the Jews in Russia to be released from that country. The bear is a symbol for Russia. I believe the Lord was touching a future call in my life.

3. **Colorado Deliverance**

   After Jim and I married, we drove to Colorado for vacation to camp out in a little pup tent. The place where we camped was beautiful, but I had trouble relaxing and enjoying it. In that wilderness location all I could think about was bears. I thought I had my fear under control until night came and we crawled into the tent. My fear of bears suddenly overwhelmed me. I was quickly becoming unglued. Finally,

I said, "Jim, I can't do this. I need some help. Please pray for me." Jim "in the Lord's name" bound the spirit of fear of bears and the spirit of fear of tornadoes and cast them out of me. After that, I never had another moment of fear concerning those issues. The enemy tried to bind me, but the Lord broke those bonds and set me free.

4.   **Breaking Off Generational Nightmares Prayer**

If you, your children, or your grandchildren, or maybe all three generations struggle with nightmares or sudden terror in the night, you can be free of the fear. The Lord does not want you to live in fear of your dreams. He wants you to receive His dream revelation. Pray this prayer:

Father, I come to You in Jesus' name. I call upon Your anointing and upon the blood of Jesus to cancel this curse. I say no to nightmares—no more bad dreams. In the name of Jesus I call for a release right now, a cutting off of generational fears. By the authority of Jesus' name I say that my sleep and the sleep of those I love will be sweet and free from torment by terror or fear. Lord, release Your redemptive work in our lives so that instead of terror we will be filled with Your Spirit in the night. I call forth Your purpose and Your destiny to be released in us, and let it unfold through our dreams. In the name of Jesus, amen.

B.   **Welcome Holy Spirit**

1.   **From Country Methodist Church to Pastor's/Prophet's Wife**

The rural Methodist church where I grew up had a typical Sunday attendance of 12-16, including our family of six. Our family did practically everything at the church. I loved God. I also loved the Holy Spirit; I just did not know how powerful He was. At that time I knew nothing about the baptism in the Holy Spirit. I just kept saying, "Holy Spirit, I want You."

2.   **Intimidation**

Jim and I met while we were both working at a hospital one summer. We became best friends and got engaged. Suddenly I was thrust into a world unlike any I had ever known. I was engaged to a man who was already moving powerfully in the gifts of the Spirit. He was prophesying over people; people were being delivered; evangelism was taking place all over the college campus. I looked at Jim and the circles he was already moving in, and I felt very intimidated. I began to feel pressure that I needed to minister to people in the same way, with the same gifting as my soon-to-be husband.

3. **Deception of Gifting vs. Relationship**

In my insecurity I began to think that giftedness equaled relationship. I felt the necessity to run by Jim any revelation I had received. If the Holy Spirit had not spoken it to Jim, I assumed that I had heard incorrectly. I discarded what the Lord had given me and went with whatever Jim thought. I began to lose my own ability to hear the Lord. Eventually the Lord began dealing with my heart on this issue. One night in a prayer meeting, I felt like the Lord had given me something to share. Just as I was about to nudge Jim with my elbow to ask if I should share it, I heard the Lord say to me, "Is he your God, or am I?" I immediately repented and realized how my hearing of God's voice had been lessened because I was placing the voice and opinion of others ahead of those of the Lord. In the same way, the area of dreams is all about relationships—most importantly, your relationship to your Father!

4. **Deliverance From Intimidation**

Years later I had a dramatic deliverance from intimidation. I continued walking farther and farther into His light and getting rid of what was hindering me from the full life God wanted for me. Since that deliverance, the Lord has used me to break off fear and intimidation from countless other lives. What a blast for God to free people from bondages similar to those you have been captive to!

C. **Life in the Basement**

1. **"I Don't Want to Hear Any More About It!"**

A few years later we were in the process of building a new house. We had to move out of our house before the new house was finished and spent three months living in another family's basement. We had four children at the time. I was homeschooling the oldest, who was six, and two of the three younger children were still in diapers. Jim was busy traveling to various conferences and meetings, speaking and doing ministry, especially on weekends. It was normal after one of these weekends for Jim to walk in the door and start talking about how the Holy Spirit had shown up in great power. While I was standing with an armload of homeschooling books, next to a load of diapers that needed folding, I said, "That's wonderful, Jim!" But inside I was saying, "I don't want to hear it. Don't tell me about another great meeting." I felt left out and shortchanged.

2. **"God, I'm Jealous!"**

The longer this went on, the more frustrated and jealous I became.

3. **"I'm the God of the Impossible!"**

One day after hearing another amazing story from Jim's latest big escapade, I leaned my head against the wall in the hallway and began to cry. I didn't even say anything; my tears were silent prayers to the Lord. He knew exactly where I was. At that moment He came to me and said, "Ann, what is impossible with man is possible with God. I am going to come and start visiting you in the night seasons."

D. **Viruses From the Pit No More!**

God had given me dreams before, but there was a significant increase in the presence of the Lord coming to me. I was like a computer infected with all sorts of bad viruses: viruses of comparison, rejection, and insufficiency. Every night the Holy Spirit came and ran His divine "spyware" to remove those viruses from the "hard drive" of my heart and mind. He did it night by night, and He did it through dream language.

II. **The Purpose of Dreams: Dream Eggs**

Night after night the Lord came to me with incredible dreams, building me up and undoing rejection, fear, and comparison. I like to call my dreams "dream eggs" because most of the time I do not receive the interpretation for them right away. Like other eggs, dream eggs need time and warmth to develop and hatch.

A. Leads to the Heart of the Father

You can receive the most awesome dream, record it in your journal, and spend hours pondering its meaning, but if it does not draw you closer to the Lord, you have missed the most important point of all.

Nighttime dreams can be extremely powerful for a couple of reasons:

1. Freedom from distractions: When we are asleep, we are free from distractions, and the Lord can have the undivided attention of our resting minds.

2. Barriers are down: The mind is powered off. All the defense mechanisms that we erect every day to protect ourselves from getting hurt are laid aside for a few hours.

B. Awakens Your Walk With Him

C. Imparts Intercessory Burdens

D. Launches You Into Ministry

E. Brings Healing

III. Are Dreams for Everybody?

Are spiritual, revelatory dreams for everybody? I believe they can be. The key is to come hungry enough to ask God to visit you in the night seasons with an expectant faith that He will answer.

A. God Gives to His Beloved, Even in Their Sleep (see Ps. 127:2).

B. Forgetting Your Dreams

Just because I don't recall a dream doesn't mean that He did not give it to me. God uses our dreams as a tool to drive us to Himself.

C. The File Cabinet

Our minds are like file cabinets. God gives us dreams in our sleep, but sometimes He files them away in the back of our mind where they are safe from being stolen by the enemy and where they can be pulled out again at an appropriate time. God never wastes anything. If He gives you a dream, He has an amazingly divine reason.

IV. Interpreting Your Dreams

A. Some Dreams Are Understood; Some Are Not

In my experience, I do not understand every dream that God gives to me. I try to allow that to draw me to Him.

B. Ask Me Again!

Having a question not answered sometimes drives you deeper to discover what it means. It's God's language saying to you, "Come a little closer and ask me again." When you are desperate, you're more attentive, your hearing gets sharper, you study...you draw closer to the Lord.

C. Your Personal Alphabet—the Importance of Journaling

If you want to know how God speaks to you, then journal. In my journals I record the dream, my ponderings about the dream, the circumstances I'm going through at that time, what I believe the application is; it ends up being more than just a dream journal. I start to see more clearly what the Lord is saying to me in my life. As I look at past journals, I can see how the Lord has walked me through and matured me. You will learn how God speaks to you through journaling.

1. The Farmhouse—the Father's House

The farmhouse I grew up in is what God uses to speak to me about my Father's house, my heavenly Father's house. I had three brothers: John, David, and Paul. God used each of my brothers as symbols for other people. My dreams weren't about them; they were about who they represented. But I wouldn't have known that if I had not journaled and seen the recurring alphabet God was using.

2. #29—God "Picked" Number 29—the Number God Assigned to Me

Scriptures of "29" significance:

- Jeremiah 29:11
- Esther 2:9
- 2 Peter 2:9

- Psalms 29
- Ruth 2:9

Reflection Questions
Lesson Five: Dreams Work!

Answers to these questions can be found in the back of the study guide.

1. Dreams can have _____ ties.

2. God wants us to view past nightmares through His _____ point of view.

3. The area of dreams is all about _____, most importantly, your _____ to your Father

4. The Lord wants you to be able to _____ people from bondages similar to those you have been captive to in the past.

5. God can remove the "_____" of comparison, rejection, and insufficiency from the "hard drive" of our hearts and minds through dream language.

6. Dreams can be compared to _____ that need time and warmth to develop and hatch.

7. What are two reasons why dreams at night can be extremely powerful?

    1)

    2)

8. What are five purposes of dreams?

    1)

    2)

    3)

    4)

    5)

9. What is one positive purpose of having a question that has not been answered?

The Diversity of Dreams

I. Diversity of Giftings

Dreams are as diverse as the languages we speak, the clothing we wear, and the food we eat. Dreams are an expression of the creative heart of God.

Revelatory dreams naturally fall under the spiritual gift of prophecy. Dreams may also be an impartation of the gift of discerning of spirits. Just as there are no clear lines of demarcation between spiritual gifts (the word of wisdom blends into a word of knowledge; the gift of faith overlaps with the workings of miracles), dreams are spiritual gifts that also intertwine.

Dream language is a dynamic, living language of love. The primary difference between dreams and other revelatory impartations is that we receive dreams first in our subconscious and only later become aware of them in our conscious minds. Because of the divine nature of revelation, we must depend on the Holy Spirit for understanding.

A. **John 16:13:** *"But when He, the Spirit of truth, comes, He will guide you into all the truth; for He will not speak on His own initiative, but whatever He hears, He will speak; and He will disclose to you what is to come."*

B. **1 Corinthians 12:4-7:** *"Now there are varieties of gifts, but the same Spirit. And there are varieties of ministries, and the same Lord. There are varieties of effects, but the same God who works all things in all persons. But to each one is given the manifestation of the Spirit for the common good."*

II. Dreams According to Your Sphere

A. Sphere of Revelation

When the Holy Spirit gives you dreams and other types of supernatural encounters, He will do so according to the calling of God on your life. You receive according to the sphere of influence you have in your life.

B.   Measure of Rule

Part of our creation mandate from God is to exercise dominion over creation. We have a stewardship to rule in the earth. Our measure of delegated rule is determined by three elements:

1.   **Measure of Faith**—the degree of confidence with which we move in our gift with authority. (See Romans 12:3.)

2.   **Measure of Gift**—the specific level or degree of grace gifting we have received from the Holy Spirit.

3.   **Measure of Authority**—our functional position and sphere of influence. (See Second Corinthians 10:13.)

III. Categories of Dreams

A.   Two Main Categories:

1.   **Dreams of Self-Disclosure**—(Sometimes called *internal* or *intrinsic*.)

This category encompasses the vast majority of our dreams. Most of your dreams are about you. God gives us personal dreams of self-disclosure in order to help us in life's journey.

2.   **Dreams of Outside Events**—(Sometimes called *external* or *extrinsic*.)

External dreams relate to your sphere of influence. Sometimes these dreams will be used to call you *to* something but not fully release or commission you into it. In this case, think of the dreams as part of your learning curve, your training in your spiritual vocabulary. He shows you a glimpse of what lies ahead in order to whet your appetite and inspire you to continue pressing forward. The most common purpose of external dreams is to draw us into intercession.

B.   Dreams From the Holy Spirit

1.   **Dreams of Destiny, Purpose, and Calling**

Destiny dreams reveal part of the progressive calling of God regarding your life, guidance, and vocation. Generally, they relate to your sphere of influence. Sometimes they will be extrinsic dreams regarding God's redemptive plan for a city, region, or nation. At times, destiny dreams are more personal, revealing the unfolding of your life in God's plan. They may relate only to the present, where you are right now, or they may deal with the past, present, and future of your life.

2. **Dreams of Edification**

Edifying dreams are inspirational in tone. They are filled with revelation, and they produce hope. (See Jacob's dream in Genesis 28.)

3. **Dreams of Exhortation**

Dreams of exhortation or "courage dreams" often contain a strong sense of urgency. They challenge us to take action. They produce faith. Dreams of exhortation also reveal an accurate, detailed picture of what is going on behind the scenes, especially in the demonic realm. This revelation is for the purpose of challenging us to take courage and act upon what we have seen.

4. **Dreams of Comfort**

Dreams of comfort help to heal our emotions and our memories. We can use them to reinterpret circumstances of our past with a heavenly lens, helping us to see things differently. Comfort dreams give us God's perspective on a situation so that we can receive emotional healing.

5. **Dreams of Correction**

Corrective dreams reveal personal changes that we need to make in order to be able to move forward. These are not condemning dreams. A corrective dream might unsettle us at first. They provoke us and stir us up; they even make us angry sometimes because our natural man does not always want to respond to the things of God. God wants to perfect us, so He sometimes uses dreams of correction.

6. **Dreams of Direction**

Directive dreams often contain a higher level of revelation and are prophetic in nature. Their purpose is to give specific guidance, which may even include warnings of some kind. Sometimes directive dreams will fill us with a desire for some spiritual quality or dimension that we do not yet possess and inspire us to begin pursuing it. Ultimately, dreams of direction serve to help us get farther down the road toward fulfilling our destiny and purpose, showing us signposts and helping us avoid pitfalls along the way. (See Matthew 2 and the dream of the wise men whom God warned not to return to Herod.)

7. **Dreams of Instruction**

Instructive dreams teach us. Scriptures are often highlighted in these dreams, and frequently you will hear a voice speaking to you. Sometimes instructive dreams will even be doctrinal in nature, but they will always contain insight with revelation. (See Job 33:14-20.)

8. **Dreams Revealing the Heart**

Dreams of self-disclosure or self-condition show us where we presently stand with God. Jeremiah 17:9 says: *"The heart is more deceitful than all else and is desperately sick; who can understand it?"* And Jesus said, *"...For out of the abundance of the heart the mouth speaks"* (Matt. 12:34b NKJV).

(See also the dream that God gave to Abimelech in Genesis 20:1-18 when he took Abraham's wife, Sarah, into his harem.)

9. **Dreams of Cleansing**

Some people call these "flushing" dreams. One of the most common images associated with the cleansing dream is that of being in the bathroom, on the toilet, or taking a shower. Cleansing dreams are used to wash us from the dust and dirt that we pick up by walking in the world. Sometimes our hearts and minds become tainted by our contact with the sin and evil in the world. Sanctifying dreams can help with that process. Essentially, these dreams are all about applying the cleansing blood of Jesus to our lives.

10. **Dreams of Spiritual Warfare**

Spiritual warfare dreams are calls to prayer that reveal hindrances that are in the way and may include calls to worship and fasting.

Their purpose is to inspire us to press through to victory by the cross of Christ, tearing down strongholds and overcoming every obstacle or barrier that stands in the way. Sometimes these dreams come in pairs and carry the same meaning to give additional insight.

11. Dreams of Creativity

Creative dreams involve such things as designs, inventions, and new ways of doing things. They can charge our spirit man and help us become change-makers, changing the culture of our homes, cities, the lives of others, and even the strongholds of our minds. God often uses creative dreams with artistic people to give them songs to sing, pictures to paint, or words to write.

12. Dreams With Impartation

Dreams of impartation are used to activate any of the various dimensions of the gifts of the Spirit. Many times these dreams will release the gift of healing, both emotional and physical. In some cases an angel of the Lord may actually appear in your room and touch you, releasing one of Heaven's power encounters.

C. Dreams From the Natural Man

1. Body Dreams

Body dreams generally arise from and reflect some aspect of the physical condition of the person who is dreaming. Just because body dreams are not necessarily spiritual does not mean that they are demonic. It is important to pay attention to body dreams because they can provide clues to changes we may need to make in our natural lives.

2. Chemical Dreams

These are sometimes known as hormone dreams and often come as a result of medications we are taking. They can reveal the need for our bodies to go through some cleansing. They may also arise because of changing or abnormal hormone or chemical levels in the body.

3. Soulish Dreams

Soulish does not necessarily mean fleshly. Soulish dreams may simply be our emotions expressing our needs or desires. They may speak to us about the need for sanctification in some area of our lives. One significant value of soulish dreams is that they can show us things about ourselves that we may otherwise fail to see when awake.

D. Dreams From the Demonic Realms

Anything that God has and uses, the enemy seeks to counterfeit, including dreams.

1. Dark Dreams

These dreams can be dark in mood and tone and also literally dark with subdued or muted colors. This lack of bright, vivid, and lively colors is one way of determining that a dream may come from a dark or even demonic source. Dark dreams commonly conjure up dark emotions and often employ dark symbols, emblems that instill a sense of discomfort or unease. There are also dark chemical dreams that are brought on as a result of involvement with witchcraft and illegal drug use. Repent, turn to the Lord, and seek help if this is the case.

2. Dreams of Fear and Panic

Most nightmares, especially childhood nightmares, fall into this category. Dreams of fear and panic often arise from trauma. Simply rebuking the fear or the panic may not be enough. It may be necessary to ask the Holy Spirit to reveal the root of the frightening dreams so that repentance, cleansing, or healing can take place. Learn to exercise your authority in Christ and ward off these haunting dreams in Jesus' name.

3. Dreams of Deception

Deceptive dreams are often the work of deceitful spirits, which Scripture says will be particularly active in the last days (see 1 Tim. 4:1). Deceptive spirits seek to draw us away from the place of security to a place of insecurity. Deceptive dreams create images and impressions in our minds that will turn us away from the true path of God's light into the darkness of error and heresy. Under the influence of deceptive dreams we can make mistakes in every area of life:

doctrine, finances, sexuality, relationships, career choices, parenting. Walking in the light of transparent relationships with other believers in the Body of Christ is ammunition that overcomes the deceptive spirit.

IV. Keeping It Simple!

A. Three Types of Dreams

1. A Simple Message Dream

In Matthew 12, Joseph understood the dreams concerning Mary and Herod. There was no real need for interpretation. These dreams were direct, to the point, and self-interpreted.

2. The Simple Symbolic Dream

Dreams can be filled with symbols. Often the symbolism is clear enough that the dreamer and others can understand it without any complicated interpretation. When Joseph was given his dream in Genesis 37, he fully understood it, as did his brothers, to the point that they wanted to kill him even though it had symbols of the sun, moon, and stars.

3. The Complex Symbolic Dream

This type of dream needs interpretative skill from someone who has the ability in the gift of interpretation or from someone who knows how to seek God to find revelation. We find this type of dream in the life of Joseph when he interprets Pharaoh's dream. In Daniel 2 and 4, we find good examples of this type of dream. In Daniel 8, we find a dream in which Daniel actually sought divine interpretation.

B. Rejoice! Dreams Are Your Inheritance

It will take time and experience to become adept at identifying different dream types and categories and interpreting the messages you receive. Relax in the assurance that God will not move you along faster than you can handle. He will gently and lovingly guide you along the way in your very own diversity of dreams.

"...He gives to His beloved even in [their] *sleep"* (Ps. 127:2).

V.   Closing Prayer

Declare with me: *You give to me, Your beloved, even in my sleep.*

Reflection Questions
Lesson Six: The Diversity of Dreams

Answers to these questions can be found in the back of the study guide.

1. Dreams are _____. They are an expression of the _____ heart of God and are the dynamic, living language of _____.

2. Because of the divine nature of _____, we must depend on the Holy Spirit for understanding.

3. John 16:13 says that the Holy Spirit will guide us into all _____.

4. The Holy Spirit will give you dreams and other types of supernatural encounters according to the _____ of _____ you have in your life.

5. Your measure of delegated rule is determined by your measure of _____, measure of _____, and measure of _____.

6. The two main categories of dreams include _____, which God gives us to _____ us in life's journey, and _____, which God uses to draw us into _____ and inspire us to press forward.

7. From Section III B, C, and D, review the types of dreams from the Holy Spirit, from natural man, and from the demonic realm. Write below the types of dreams that you have experienced.

8. The best thing you can remember when it comes to the diversity of dreams is to keep it _____!

9. The three types of dreams are the simple _____, the simple _____, and the _____ _____.

10. Write out below the number one insight you gained from this lesson and how you desire to apply it to your life.

LESSON SEVEN

Understanding the Dreams You Dream

I. Where Do I Start?

Does understanding and interpreting dreams seem like a giant maze with no apparent end in sight? Take comfort! Others throughout the ages have felt the same way! But the Lord has a word for us: "I will be your Helper!"

A. Help for the Helpless!

1. **John 14:16:** *"I will ask the Father, and He will give you another **Helper**, that He may be with you forever;"* (emphasis added).

2. **John 14:26:** *"But the **Helper**, the Holy Spirit, whom the Father will send in My name, He will teach you all things, and bring to your remembrance all that I said to you"* (emphasis added).

3. **John 15:26:** *"When the **Helper** comes, whom I will send to you from the Father, that is the Spirit of truth who proceeds from the Father, He will testify about Me,"* (emphasis added).

4. **John 16:7:** *"But I tell you the truth, it is to your advantage that I go away; for if I do not go away, the **Helper** will not come to you; but if I go, I will send Him to you"* (emphasis added).

B. Our Personal Tutor

1. **John 16:13-15:** *"But when He, the Spirit of truth, comes, He will guide you into all the truth; for He will not speak on His own initiative, but whatever He hears, He will speak; and He will disclose to you what is to come. He will glorify Me, for He will take of Mine and will disclose it to*

you. All things that the Father has are Mine; therefore I said that He takes of Mine and will disclose it to you."

2. **From *The Beginner's Guide to Hearing God* by James W. Goll**

"The Holy Spirit is our counselor and our teacher, yet He is more than a teacher—more like a tutor. But He is not just any tutor; He's the kind who truly loves to spend individual, personal time with each of His students. He is like that rare kind of guidance counselor who actually becomes a friend. He is like the teacher who becomes a personal mentor. As a personal Tutor, He is also a personal coach to help us win out on the playing field of life.

"In addition—great news!—He's not like an ordinary tutor or teacher who clocks in and out. As we graduate from one level of spiritual development to the next, he remains our lifetime personal Tutor. We start with the best, and we end with the best. As we end our days here on earth, He even prepares us for our post-graduate course in life hereafter! All along, He individually instructs us as to what life lessons we need to learn, and in what order to take them."[1]

C. Ask and You Will Receive!

1. **James 1:5-8:** *"But if any of you lacks wisdom, let him ask of God, who gives to all generously and without reproach, and it will be given to him. But he must ask in faith without any doubting, for the one who doubts is like the surf of the sea, driven and tossed by the wind. For that man ought not to expect that he will receive anything from the Lord, being a double-minded man, unstable in all his ways."*

2. **James 4:2:** *"…You do not have because you do not ask."*

3. **Matthew 7:8:** *"For everyone who asks receives, and he who seeks finds, and to him who knocks it will be opened."*

II. The Most Common Dreams People Have

Various ministries and organizations have logged thousands of dreams and therefore have been able to decipher the most common dreams people have. The following is a partial listing of these most common types of dreams. This list is not comprehensive, and the dreams are not listed in any certain order.

A. **Dreams of Your House**

The house normally represents the individual's life, and the circumstances taking place in the house reflect specific activity in the person's life. These dreams may represent a church as well.

B. **Dreams of Going to School**

Often these dreams center around the taking of tests. This can be a dream of going through a test for the purpose of promotion. You might find yourself searching for your next class—guidance is needed; or classes might need to be retaken—tests were failed in the past, and an opportunity is being given to learn from past failures. High school dreams can be a sign that you are enrolled in the School of the Holy Spirit, etc.

C. **Dreams of Various Vehicles**

These may indicate the calling a person has, the vehicle of purpose that will carry them from one point to another. Cars, planes, buses, etc., may be symbols of the type and even size of the ministry a person is or will be engaged in.

D. **Dreams Concerning Storms**

These are often hints of things that are on the horizon—both dark negative storms of demonic attack for the purpose of prayer and showers of blessings that are imminent.

E. **Dreams of Flying**

These dreams deal with the spiritual capacity to rise above problems and difficulties and to soar into the heavenlies. These are some of the most inspirational in tone of all dreams.

F. **Dreams of Being Naked or Exposed**

These dreams indicate the dreamer will be or is becoming transparent and vulnerable. This may be exhilarating or fearful.

G. **Dreams of the Condition of Your Teeth**

Often, these dreams reveal the need for wisdom. Are your teeth loose, rotten, falling out, bright and shining, etc.?

H.   Dreams of Past Relationships

These might indicate that the person is being tempted to fall back into old patterns and ways of thinking. Depending on whom the person is in the dream and what he or she represents to you—these dreams might also be an indication of the need to renew your former desires and godly passions for good things in life.

I.   Dreams of Dying

These dreams are not normally literal about the person seen in the dream but are symbolic about something that is passing away or departing from your life. The type of death may be important to note. Watch to see though if resurrection is on the other side.

J.   Dreams of Births

Normally these dreams are not about an actual childbirth, but rather about new seasons of purpose and destiny coming forth into the life of the dreamer. If a name is given to the child—pay close attention.

K.   Dreams of Taking a Shower

These are cleansing type dreams (toilets, showers, bathtubs, etc.) revealing things that are in process of being flushed out of your life, cleansed and flushed away, etc.

L.   Dreams of Falling

These dreams may reveal that there is a fear of losing control of some area of life or that you are getting free of directing your own life. What the person falls into in the dream is a major key to proper understanding. The outstanding primary emotions in these dreams will indicate which way to interpret them.

M.   Dreams of Chasing and Being Chased

These dreams often reveal enemies that are at work coming against your life and purpose. Or on the opposite side—they may indicate the passionate pursuit of God in your life and you towards Him. Again, the emotion will often determine the direction of interpretation.

N. Dreams of Relatives Alive and Dead

These dreams probably indicate generational issues at work in your life—both blessings and curses. Discernment will be needed on whether to accept the blessing or cut off the darkness. This is particularly true if grandparents appear in your dreams as they will indicate generational issues.

O. Dreams Called Nightmares

These dreams tend to be more frequent with children or new believers in Christ. They may reveal generational enemies at work that need to be cut off.

P. Dreams of Snakes

This is possibly the most common of all of the categories of animal dreams. These dreams reveal the serpent—the devil with His demonic hosts—at work through accusation, lying, attacks, etc. Other common dreams of this nature include dreams of spiders, bears, alligators, etc.

Q. Dreams of Dogs and Cats

This is one of the other most frequent categories of dreams with animals—dogs. This symbol will indicate friendship, loyalty, protection, and good feelings. Dreams with dogs may also reveal the dark side including growling, attacking, biting, etc. These dreams could reveal a friend who is about to betray you. Dreams with cats are also quite common. These dreams also vary in nature with everything from the feeling of being loved, to being smothered, to persnickety attitudes, to occultic sexual activity.

R. Dreams of Going Through Doors

These dreams reveal change that is coming. New ways, new opportunities, new advancements are on the way. Similar to dreams of doors are also dreams including elevators, escalators, etc. You are coming up higher in your purpose and calling.

S. Dreams of Clocks and Watches

These dreams reveal what time it is in the dreamer's life or the need for a wake-up call in the Body of Christ or in a nation. It is time to be alert and watchful. These dreams might indicate a Scripture verse as well giving a deeper message.

T. **Dreams With Scripture Verses**

Bible passages might appear indicating messages from God. This phenomenon may occur in a number of ways: verbal quotations, digital clock readouts, a dramatization of a scene from the Bible, etc. These are often watchmen type dreams—dreams of instruction filled with the ways of wisdom.

Endnote

1. James W. Goll, *The Beginner's Guide to Hearing God* (Ventura, CA: Regal Books, 2004)

Reflection Questions
Lesson Seven: Understanding the Dreams You Dream

Answers to these questions can be found in the back of the study guide.

1. John 14:26 says *"But the _____, the Holy Spirit, whom the Father will send in My name, He will teach you all things, and bring to your remembrance all that I said to you."*

2. The Holy Spirit is our _____ and _____. He is our personal _____.

3. Matthew 7:8 declares that those who _____ will receive.

4. From Section II, review the 20 most common dreams people have. If you have experienced these types of dreams, list six different types you have had. Circle those that have been the most impacting to you.

    _____   _____

    _____   _____

    _____   _____

5. For one of the dreams you circled above, consider if you have increased your understanding about that dream as a result of this lesson. Briefly write out that dream below and any understanding gained.

6. Write below two primary insights you gained from this lesson. Then spend a short time in prayer around those two points, asking the Lord to implant those messages in your heart.

Properly Interpreting Dreams

I. Where Are the Josephs and Daniels for Our Day?

A. An Experience in Germany

When traveling by train from the Frankfurt, Germany, region to Rossenheim in southern Bavaria in the middle of the night, I kept hearing the Holy Spirit speak to me over and over, "Where are the Daniels, the Josephs, and the Esthers?"

As I have pondered deeply on this word for years, I believe the Holy Spirit is searching. Yes, He is on a quest to find believers who dream dreams at any cost, have a discerning spirit to properly interpret the times, and who learn to intercede out of a posture of revelation.

Where are the Josephs and Daniels for this generation? Perhaps some of them are those listening to this message and studying to show themselves approved as workmen for God.

B. Interpretations Belong to God!

1. **From the Life of Joseph—Genesis 40:8:** *"Then they said to him, 'We have had a dream and there is no one to interpret it.' Then Joseph said to them, 'Do not interpretations belong to God? Tell it to me, please.'"*

2. **From the Life of Daniel—Daniel 1:17, 20:** *"As for these four youths, God gave them knowledge and intelligence in every branch of literature and wisdom; Daniel even understood all kinds of visions and dreams. As for every matter of wisdom and understanding about which the king consulted*

them, he found them ten times better than all the magicians and conjurers who were in all his realm."

3. **From the Life of Issachar—1 Chronicles 12:32:** *"Of the sons of Issachar, men who understood the times, with knowledge of what Israel should do, their chiefs were two hundred; and all their kinsmen were at their command."*

4. **In the Body of Christ—1 Corinthians 12:7-8:** *"But to each one is given the manifestation of the Spirit for the common good. For to one is given the word of wisdom through the Spirit, and to another the word of knowledge according to the same Spirit."*

5. Concluding thought: What God did before, He wants to do again! Right here—right now!

II. **Basic Points for Interpreting Dreams**

A. **Review—Revelation Is Full of Symbolism!**

As dreams, visions, and revelations are full of symbolism, they need to be viewed much the same as parables. Ask the Lord to show you the central issue. When dreams, etc., are broken down into too many details, the meaning becomes increasingly obscure. Frame it out like a giant jigsaw puzzle; then the rest of the pieces will fall into place and the picture will be seen.

Dreams are often the language of emotions and therefore contain much symbolism. We must learn to take our interpretations first from Scripture, and then from our own lives. God is consistent with His symbolic language. How He spoke in Genesis will be similar to the symbols and types in the Book of Revelation. This holds true in our own lives as well.

B. **Three Realms for Interpretation of Symbols**

1. The first place to look is in **Scripture.** The Bible is full of parables and allegories from which to draw types, shadows, and symbols. Examples include the mustard seed being faith, incense being the prayers of the saints, seed representing the Word of God, and the candlesticks being the Church.

2. Dream symbols are often **colloquial expressions** which fill our memory banks. They become turned into pictorial language by the Holy Spirit. God takes the "sayings" and idioms and uses them to speak spiritual truth.

   An example is Gideon in Judges 7:9-15 in which a barley cake appears. Gideon grew up as a thresher of wheat and barley. The barley cake therefore was a symbol from his colloquial spiritual alphabet with distinct meaning to him.

3. The third realm of symbols comes from our own **personal revelatory alphabet**. In this case, the object or symbol does not mean the same to you as it would to others. Such as

   a. **Animals, birds, and fish.** Isaiah—the Messiah is presented as a *Lamb* to slaughter. John—Jesus is *Shepherd*, and disciples are presented as little *lambs*. Revelation—the *Lamb* is now a Conqueror.

   b. **People** who appear in our dreams can be interpreted on three levels: 1) Literal, 2) Symbolic, 3) Meaning of the name. Ask yourself: What does the person represent to me? What is the outstanding characteristic of the individual?

   c. **Birth and death** can be interpreted on three levels: 1) Literal, 2) What you care for is growing or dying, 3) It is spiritual—a new beginning.

   d. **Children's dreams.** What do you do with nightmares? At times we need to simply rebuke the devourer. Other times we need to cleanse the house. Yet on other occasions we must pray and ask the Lord for the root issue, and we must deal with it accordingly.

   e. **Sexual dreams.** 1) Cleansing the house of defilement of flesh and spirit, 2) Portraying a call into intimacy, 3) Revealing desire/passion—natural issues of life.

C. Seek the Wisdom Ways of God!
From *Dream* by Mark Rutland

"Believers must, of course, be cautious when seeking to understand dreams and even more prudent when acting on them. There is no substitute for wisdom and discernment in dream interpretation, and prayer is crucial to developing them. Believers should commit their subconscious minds to the Lord as well as their waking thoughts, and then seek from God, in earnest prayer, understanding for the visions of the night."[1]

1. Visual vs. Actual

Insights, revelations, warnings, and prophecies from the Lord may come in supernatural *visual* dreams or in *actual* dreams. (Read *The Seer* by James W. Goll for more details on this subject.)

a. Visual Dreams

These *visual* revelations do not have as much of an active participation of the person's spirit/soul as an *actual* visitation from the Lord. The person simply observes and receives the message.

These visual dreams may contain more symbols, mysteries, and obscurities than do other types of revelation.

b. Actual Dreams

These supernatural *actual* dreams are those in which God's tangible presence is evident in some way. To *see* the Lord in a dream is *visual*, but for the Lord to *manifest* Himself to you in a dream is *actual*.

If you dream something angelic, and you sense that same presence when you wake up, it was more than just a *visual symbolic* dream. The angels were *actually* there. But if there was no manifested presence when you awoke, then the dream was simply *visual*, though it may still contain a message from God.

A manifestation of blessing, healing, deliverance, or endowment of power requires an *actual* visitation from the Lord in some form. Such manifestations involve an impartation of God's anointing which will manifest in the natural realm. Therefore, an *actual impartation* occurs, and the person actively participates though his or her body is asleep.

III. Major Points for Greater Understanding

A. Reduce the Dream to Its Simplest Form

1. **With Too Much Detail** you will lose the interpretation. Keep it simple—too much detail obscures the meaning—take the dream to the simplest form and build on that.

2. **Context Determines Interpretation.** The meaning is not always the same. An example: a seed can mean faith, the Word, the Kingdom of God, a future harvest, etc. There are no steadfast formulas. According to First Corinthians 2:14 the things of the spirit are spiritually discerned—not naturally discerned.

3. **Scenes of Dreams or Repetitious Dreams.** Is it four dreams or is it different aspects of the same issue? More than one dream in the same night is often a different look or version of the same message.

4. **The First Questions to Ask**

   a. **Are You Observing?**

   Where are you in the dream? If you are in the observation mode, then the dream is not about you. It is about someone or somewhere else. God does nothing without a witness observing issues.

   b. **Are You Participating?**

   Are you participating but still not the main figure? This dream is not about you as the central figure, but includes you.

   c. **Are You the Focus?**

   Is everyone watching you? This dream is about you as the central figure of the dream.

5. **What Are the Objects, Thoughts, and Emotions in the Dream?**

   Are there words in the dream? What impressions and thoughts are you left with when you are awakened or recall the dream? What is the intensity of the dream—the main emotion? You will know intuitively what the more important issues are.

6. **Symbolic Colors**

Colors can have both a good or positive meaning as well as a bad or negative meaning. Context is the key! Dreams are full of these understandings—they are often descriptive parables of light. Some examples are:

a. **Amber**—glory of God (see Ezek. 1:4; 8:2 NKJV).

b. **Black**—sin, death, and famine (see Lam. 4:8; Rev. 6:5).

c. **Blue**—heaven; Holy Spirit (see Num. 15:38).

d. **Crimson/Scarlet**—blood atonement; sacrifice (see Isa. 1:18; Lev.14:52; Josh. 2:18,21).

e. **Purple**—kingship; royalty (see John 19:2; Judg. 8:26).

f. **Red**—bloodshed; war (see Rev. 6:4; 12:3; 2 Kings 3:22).

g. **White**—purity, light, righteousness (see Rev. 6:2; 7:9; 19:8).

7. **Basic Principles of Interpretation of Numbers**

If you follow these principles, you will be preserved from error and extremes.

a. The simple numbers of 1-13 often have spiritual significance.

b. Multiples of these numbers, or doubling or tripling, carries basically the same meaning, only they intensify the truth.

c. The first use of the number in Scripture generally conveys its spiritual meaning.

d. Consistency of interpretation: God is consistent, and what a number means in Genesis, it will mean through all Scripture to Revelation.

e. The spiritual significance is not always stated, but may be veiled, hidden, or seen by comparison with other Scriptures.

f. Generally there are good and evil, true and counterfeit, godly and satanic aspects in numbers.

8. **Individual Numbers and Their Possible Symbolic Meanings**

   a. **One**—God, beginning, source (see Gen. 1:1; John 1:1-3).

   b. **Two**—witness, testimony (see John 8:17; Matt. 18:16; Deut. 17:6).

   c. **Three**—Godhead, divine completeness (see Ezek. 14:14-18; Dan. 3:23-24).

   d. **Four**—earth, creation, winds, seasons (see Gen. 2:10; Mark 16:15; 1 Cor. 15:39).

   e. **Five**—cross, grace, atonement (see Gen. 1:20-23; Lev. 1:5; Eph. 4:11).

   f. **Six**—man, beast, satan (see Gen. 1:26-31; 1 Sam. 17:4,7; Num. 35:15).

   g. **Seven**—perfection, completeness (see Heb. 6:1-2; Jude 14; Josh. 6).

   h. **Eight**—new beginning (see Gen. 17:12; 1 Pet. 3:20; 2 Pet. 3:8).

   i. **Nine**—finality, fullness (see Matt. 27:45; Gen. 7:1-2; Gal. 5:22; 1 Cor. 12:1-12).

   j. **Ten**—law, government (see Gen. 1; Dan. 2; Exod. 34:28).

   k. **Eleven**—disorganization, lawlessness, antichrist (see Dan. 7:24; Gen. 32:22).

   l. **Twelve**—divine government, apostolic fullness (see Exod. 28:21; Matt. 10:2-5; Lev. 24:5-6).

   m. **Thirteen**—rebellion, backsliding, apostasy (see Gen. 14:4; 10:10; 1 Kings 11:6).

   (Refer to the book *Interpreting the Symbols and Types* by Kevin Conner.)

9. **The Cultural Interpretive Process**

West vs. East—American instead of British—Israel—India—New Zealand. There are cultural and social interpretations that must also be brought into our understanding. The sphere of one's influence determines how much one must consider these things.

10. **Meditating on the Laws of God**

See Psalms 63:6, 77:12, 119:15, 143:5. We must gain understanding of the principles or metaphors of Scripture—meditate on them day and night. They can have layers of meaning!

IV. Keeping Interpretation Simple

A. Summary of Things to Remember

1. Most of all, dreams should be interpreted on a personal basis first (see John 10:3).

2. Most dreams should not be taken literally. They need interpretation (see Dan. 1:17; Gen. 40:8).

3. God will use familiar terms you know (see Matt. 4:19).

4. Ponder on the dream or revelation and ask the Holy Spirit for insight (see Dan. 7:8; 8:15-16; Luke 2:19; 1 Cor. 2:10-12).

5. Ask the Holy Spirit what the certain thought, word, or issue is in the revelation. Reduce the dream to its simplest form. What is the main thought? What object or thought occurs most often? Frame it out like a giant jigsaw puzzle. Once you get the frame, the rest of it will fit together. What is the central *rhema* word? Not all the details are important or have meaning.

6. Search it out in the Word. Dreams from the Lord will never go against His Word (see Prov. 25:2).

7. What did you sense and feel from the dream? Was there a good or evil presence? What was the primary emotion? Fear, love, concern, hopelessness, disappointment?

8. Relate the dreams to your circumstances and spheres of influence.

9. Consecutive dreams often have the same or similar meaning (see Gen. 41:1-7;25-32). God will speak the same message more than once.

10. What are the colors? Is everything black and white with one main object in color?

11. Interpretations can be on three levels:

    a. Personal

    b. Church

        i. Congregation

        ii. City

        iii. Church in a

        iv. Global Body of Christ

    c. National and International—these can be governmental in nature.

12. More than one interpretation can come forth from one dream. Just as with Scripture, there is the historical context as well as the personal, present implication. So it is with dreams, etc. It might be a general word for the Church with specific applications for yourself (or others).

13. Some dreams may only be understood in the future. They unfold over time. Details will make sense down the road.

14. Write down the summary, the date, your location, the time (if you woke up from it), the main emotions, and a possible interpretation in a journal.

15. The key to proper interpretation is question, question, question. (See Zechariah 4 as an example of how to respond to a revelatory experience. Humility is marked by being teachable.)

B. Dreams Are Significant to All!

"There couldn't be a society of people who didn't dream. They'd be dead in two weeks." *William Burroughs*

"To receive a dream is the human obligation that begins to move the divine purpose from the mind of God to become reality in human history." *Mark Rutland*

Dreams are where space and time are pushed away, where God allows our inner selves to see beyond and behind the conscious plane and where possibilities and hopes, as well as all our hidden monsters, come out, come out wherever they are.

"Dreaming permits each and every one of us to be quietly and safely insane every night of our lives." *Charles William Dement*

C. **Life Is More Than Dreams!**
    From *Dream* by Mark Rutland

"If we idolize that primary mental image and cling to it too tenaciously, we may well despise the realization of the dream when it finally arrives. An overly cherished fantasy has the capacity to steal our joy and even blind us to the dream for which we have longed."[2]

Ecclesiastes 5:7 says not to base your life on dreams alone! *"For in many dreams and in many words there is emptiness* [vanity]*—Rather, fear God!"*

Endnotes

1. Mark Rutland, *Dream: Awake or Asleep, Unlock the Power of God's Vision* (Lake Mary, FL: Charisma House, 2003).

2. Ibid.

Reflection Questions
Lesson Eight: Properly Interpreting Dreams

Answers to these questions can be found in the back of the study guide.

1. What God did in the life of Joseph, Daniel, and in the sons of Issachar, He wants to do _____ .

2. Dreams, visions, and revelations are full of _____; they need to be viewed much the same as _____ .

3. List the three realms for interpretation of symbols:

4. To see the Lord in a dream is _____, but for the Lord to *manifest* Himself to you in a dream is _____ .

5. It's best to reduce the dream to its _____ form.

6. From Section III, review the 10 Major Points for Greater Understanding. Think of a dream that you have had and seek to understand it in more depth by applying a few of these points. Record your insights below.

7. From Section IV A, review the Summary of Things to Remember. List below five keys of interpretation that the Holy Spirit is highlighting for you to remember and apply.

8. What is the danger of idolizing that primary mental image of a dream or vision and clinging to it too tenaciously?

PART 3

WALKING
IN
WISDOM

LESSON NINE

Stops Along the Way

By Michal Ann Goll

I. **Dreams Delivered By Angels—Actual Experiences**

A. **Kansas City Activation**

This dream occurred years ago while we were still living in Kansas City. We had been through an incredible amount of spiritual warfare. It was a very dark and very difficult period in our lives. During this time Jim got very sick. One day I started feeling ill as well. At times my fever ran as high as 104 or 105 degrees.

Even my doctor did not know what was going on at first. Eventually I was hospitalized with a very unusual kind of double pneumonia that had settled in the upper part of my lungs. The pneumonia was so severe that I spent two weeks in the hospital. We had to ship our young children out to be cared for by family. I was away from my children for about six weeks!

When I came home from the hospital, I was so weak that I could barely lift a coffee mug. This was only a few days before a major conference that we were planning to attend. One morning I had a dream where an oppressor was trying to get everyone to turn away from Jesus. I was one of the leaders of this Jesus group. My life was being threatened. If I refused to renounce Jesus, I could be killed. I turned and looked at the people in my group, knowing that my decision would affect how they responded. We all stood up and started singing a song to Jesus. At that point an enemy soldier came over and struck me on the top of the head with the butt of his rifle. When this happened in the dream, there was an actual experience outside of the dream. It was like the dream opened the doorway for the next step, and as the dream ended, I entered into the following experience. Instantly, my head "split open" figuratively from shafts of revelation light. I sat up in bed, fully aware that an angel was present in my room. It was four in the morning, yet I was totally energized with what I can only describe as circles and circles of revelation light. I was so activated that I could not stay in bed. I jumped up, not even knowing what to do with myself.

I was totally wired from the download of this dream which involved a word that I was supposed to give to Daniel Brymer, the leader of the worship team of the church that was hosting the upcoming conference. I had this feeling of *knowing* that the members of the worship team were to be like warplanes that God was going to send to drop bombs on the enemy's territory. I felt an overwhelming sense of urgency to call, but it was too early in the morning. At an appropriate hour I phoned Daniel and told him about my dream. I said, "You are like warplanes. Your whole team is going to go up into the heavens and drop bombs of praise." He received all this with great excitement.

The Lord used this experience to launch that worship team into a higher plane of purpose and anointing. All the praise and worship music at that conference was recorded and the resulting tapes are some of the most anointed warfare praise and worship that I have ever heard. Despite my illness, I was able to attend that first night's meeting.

B. Moravian Falls

While I was at Moravian Falls to spend some quiet time with the Lord, I stayed at the same cabin Bobby Conner had been in the week before. At the time I knew nothing of his supernatural experience, but I had a very similar experience. In the middle of the night an angel came, and I saw a map of the world on the wall. The angel had a wine bottle and smashed the wine bottle on the wall. The angel had a scroll that he unfolded and showed me a long list of people, ministries, cities, and strategies for what the Lord was going to do. I was able to read the entire scroll; then the scroll rolled back up.

II. Seeds Planted

A. Becoming Pregnant With Holy Seeds

I have had many major "destiny" dreams. These dreams are like God impregnating you with holy seeds so that you give birth to things in the Spirit. God loves to use language that we know and understand. What better analogy is there than looking at the incubation period of gestation of our own children? When the announcement of that cherished and anticipated birth is first given, our natural question is, "What will this baby look like? Will he/she look like the mother or the father?" These same questions apply to burdens/births we help to carry through dreams and intercession. We never know what those holy seeds will grow up to look like. We never know in advance where they will take us.

B. Seeds of Burden Bearing

Dreams of destiny enlarge our heart and our perspective. Our identity expands beyond ourselves until we identify with the entire world. I like to call these "seeds of burden bearing." The following are some of these impacting dreams. My main purpose in sharing these dreams is just to let the dreams unfold and let the Spirit of God stir you as He desires.

1. The World's Heartbeat

This dream came to me on March 31, 1989. In my dream, nuclear war had taken place, and even though it was a "limited" war, damage and exposure to radiation were extensive. Members of my family had been exposed to radiation and some had actually died. Like everyone else, I too had been exposed and was expected to become terminally ill. Yet somehow I escaped harm.

The scene changed and I became aware that the earth was in imminent danger of total destruction unless we interceded in prayer long enough and hard enough. The problem was getting others to respond. I remember looking out a window at night when suddenly a shuddering vibration swept through the house. I thought, *This is it!* It was not a bomb but some sort of super aircraft powerful enough and fast enough to circle the globe from north to south and wrap it with an invisible cord so strong that as it tightened, it would literally cut the world in two, plunging it into everlasting destruction.

I felt the earth collapsing underneath my feet. As I fell, I saw the earth in its normal position and heard a steady heartbeat. A moment later, the earth split and the heartbeat stopped. I saw a woman ready to give birth floating on her back in space. She was lamenting uncontrollably. Her abdomen had been opened somehow, as if by an explosion, and she held in her hands the small bloody earth. It was as though she had been unable to carry it to full term and now it was dead.

Once again the scene changed. We were in a large city at nighttime, and the threat of missile attack was imminent. Suddenly there was a flash. We could see the missile chasing us, and it was as though somehow we were riding on a missile of our own, trying to get away. Somehow, we escaped detection, and the missile lost its target. We celebrated, laughed, and danced in the relief that it was all over. This is probably a dream of end-time magnitude. It is surely a dream calling His people to spiritual warfare!

2. The War in Iraq—February 1991

During Operation Desert Storm, I had a dream where I saw part of a map of Iraq with two dotted lines coming down from the top to form a "V" toward Baghdad. I thought possibly that they represented two roads that led to Baghdad, but Jim thought they symbolized the Tigris and the Euphrates rivers and the point where they converge. I observed a Jeep-like vehicle carrying four people racing down the road trying to reach the airport at the convergence point in order to escape Iraq. The phrase came to me that they had to go through Iran to get there. I believe it was a play on words *I ran*. Before they could make good their escape, however, a military vehicle appeared behind them with a light flashing on the top.

Suddenly I was no longer just an observer but was in the Jeep with them. Immediately I began crying out to the Lord to destroy the enemy so that no harm would come to us. Before long the enemy vehicle ran off the road, turned over, and was destroyed.

Finally, the Jeep reached the end of the road, but the passengers found no airport. I was in observer mode once again. The passengers decided that a plane was coming at a certain time to airlift them out. Little did they know that only a few hundred feet away hundreds of Iraqi troops were huddled in trenches. The Iraqis captured them, brought them into a room, and told them that the only way the four of them would be set free was if one of them volunteered to allow the Iraqis to place some sort of chemical acid on his or her hand. One of the women agreed. The Iraqi leader advised her to look at the other people in the room before she made her final decision. As I watched the scene, I noticed several people whose faces were horribly altered. Their skin was ashen gray and hung so loosely on their faces that all you could see were their expressionless eyes and long thin mouths.

At this sight, the female volunteer changed her mind. But the soldiers grabbed her, held her down by force, and told her they were going to put acid on her face. She was terrified, but it turned out to be only water. This was mental torture, all part of the spirit of terror that was being released. The soldiers did actually put some acid on the inner calf of one man's right leg. His skin grew white and swollen and they promised him release, as he had fulfilled the requirement for someone to volunteer.

Finally the plane arrived, but they had to walk a long distance to get to it, which was extremely difficult for the man with the acid-burned leg to do. They made him walk up a long flight of stairs and down a long walk to the plane. When he was almost there, they closed the door in his face. He stood at the door, pounding with his fist and demanding that they let him in, which they finally did. The plane finally took off, yet there was no assurance that they were safe because the Iraqis had no air cover. The allied forces did not know who was on the plane and would surely try to bring it down. I never saw the plane crash; it simply disappeared over the horizon.

For me, the dream was a major call to prayer. My vision of that plane kept me continually before the Lord on behalf of our soldiers and everyone caught up in that conflict. Jim, under the Lord's direction, had set aside his normal schedule for the entire period of the Gulf War. For that entire month our lives were on pause, and we were watchers on the wall.

3. Three Jewish Men

In this dream, three tall, black-bearded Jewish men stood in front of me with their arms folded, saying, "Who do you think you are that God would use you to bring good news to the Jewish people? You are nothing, a nobody." I looked at them and replied, "You're absolutely right. I am a nobody. It is only by the grace of God and by His anointing that anybody does anything."

I then began praying to the Lord, and a spirit of supplication came over me. "Oh Lord," I cried out, "please release Your anointing so that the good news can be released. Only You can do this, Lord. Please shine down Your revelation light." Immediately, a light from Heaven shone down on me like a spotlight, plainly visible for everyone to see. The three Jewish men took a step back, clapped their hands to their mouths, and said, "Oh, we see!" It was as if they suddenly saw the favor of the Lord on me and changed their position.

This was a dream of destiny and calling. God does want to use us to bring good news to the Jewish people, but for me this dream was all about taking the low road and saying, "You're right. I am nobody; I am nothing." The Lord has used this approach many times to teach me how to do spiritual warfare. You don't go head-to-head with the enemy. You recognize that you are nobody, and then you simply exalt Jesus.

4. Shackles Transformed

In another dream I saw shackles on Jews' ankles coming off and being transformed into beautifully and intricately carved ivory bracelets. Basically that was it. There is no standard or formula for length of revelatory dreams. Some are quite lengthy while others are nothing more than "snapshots." God wants to change all our shackles into tokens of His bridal adornment. He can turn anything around!

5. The Well-Blended Woman

This is a dream first related to me years ago by Penny Kaeding, a personal friend who also has a ministry that is associated with ours. This was a dream that the Lord gave to Penny about me. Penny describes her dream experience as it is told from my viewpoint:

I saw oil refineries burning all over the world. I was involved in visiting these different places, handing out blankets and food. Before long, I became so overwhelmed with the crushing need of the people that I did not know what to do. In the end I was thrown into this big blender, and it was turned on. I guess it evened out all my "lumps" or something, because I came out smooth. The phrase that I heard in my dream was that I was a "well-blended woman" who was no longer overwhelmed but used by God to release His goodness, blessings, and mercy. This was years before I ever had even a thought about a ministry of compassion, years before I had any idea that I would be involved in some way in working with relief.

Although this dream is a calling dream, it is a teaching or instructional dream as well. We are all called to be well-blended believers bringing many ingredients together for His name's sake.

6. Civil War

The context of this dream was the farmhouse where I was raised, according to my personal alphabet, the Father's house, or God's house. I saw two men who seemed to represent two different armies. One man was lying on the floor in my bedroom. The bed was high enough so he could see under the bed and across the room through the door to the stairway landing. He was watching for his enemy whom he knew would be coming through David and Paul's old bedroom. (David and Paul were my brothers. Each represented something special in my personal alphabet. Paul represented the prophetic movement, specifically Paul Cain. David represented Mike Bickle and the Heart of David and worship. My other brother John represented John Wimber, the Vineyard, and healing.)

An enemy was in the Father's house coming through David and Paul's bedroom. The man lying on the floor knew he only had a split second to see his enemy and shoot his gun. Both men had the same kind of weapon. I felt the tension, sweat, strain, and anxiety of the man in my room, afraid to get even slightly tired and miss the opportunity to shoot his enemy. Quickly the other man rounded the corner and began to head down the stairs. The man in my room saw him and fired, but missed. A part of the gun fell onto the floor and alerted the man on the stairs. He turned around and began to look into my room for his enemy. Meanwhile, the man who fired the gun frantically tried to put his gun back together knowing that the man would shoot him if he found him. Whoever got his gun ready and located the enemy first would be the winner. Which one would win and which would be shot? The phrase I heard was, "Civil War."

7. **Baby Jesus**

In this dream, Jim and I seemed to be in Israel. All around us were narrow dusty roads and passageways, stone houses built together and connected in a line, separated only by stone walls. Jim seemed heartsick; he wanted to talk to people about Jesus but was so moved by what he saw that he could not participate in any conversations.

The scene shifted and it was as though we had gone back in time. An army of foot and horse soldiers was ready to march into the city. A sense of panic filled the air. People were scurrying everywhere, trying to get out of the city before it was captured. Most had already fled, but Jim and I were staying. We were dressed in old garments, long robes as in biblical times. It seemed we had no place to go; besides, we felt that we were supposed to stay. We were just sitting there in our little stone house, waiting for the enemy to enter the city.

I walked over to the window. As I looked out, a horse-drawn cart in the street below was just passing in front of our house. The people in the cart appeared to be fleeing and needed refuge. I called to them from the window, "Master, wait, wait!" The cart was moving so fast that by the time I spoke, it had already traveled past our place. I thought the occupants had not heard me. But then I heard the hoof beats slowing down. I saw the cart stop, turn around, and come back to our house. A man and a woman got off the cart and came into our house and sat down. The woman was holding a small bundle. As she sat down, she opened the bundle, and I saw that it was the baby Jesus.

8. Gang Leaders

I had this dream on January 28, 1994. I dreamt I was in a large meeting in the front of the auditorium. An angel came, lifted me up, and moved me in the air. I saw different scenes. We were near an apartment complex and a gang leader was known to be close by. As we walked in front of the complex, I looked up at the second-story balcony, saw two young men, and automatically knew the name of one of them (I had a word of knowledge). I called out his name. He was the gang leader, and he owned the apartment. Both of the men were surprised and began to shake, repenting under the conviction and power of God. A few other men walking near us in the parking lot began to shake as well. I called out to them, "Do you want to know Jesus?" They said, "Yes!" Jim said to me, "Oh, that's good!"

In another scene, I am handed a cell phone and am about to talk to a man. I immediately know that this man is living in adultery. I confront him on the phone, and he repents. (In my journal I made a note that during the night my hands were going numb as I was lying in bed.)

9. "My Body Is a Dismembered Body!"

This dream occurred on October 28, 1989. I was in a small country church, much like the little Methodist church where I grew up. The service was in progress, and I saw myself lying on a pew with a pillow and blanket, sick from pregnancy. As the service continued, a huge windstorm gradually began to overtake us. Eventually, we were completely surrounded and enveloped by this storm. Even as the wind grew, I sensed a tremendous spirit of prophecy coming upon me and filling me. I had no fear of what was going on around me because the Word of the Lord was coming forth from me and I could see His purpose in this storm.

By this time in the dream I was no longer sick and had no fear of death or harm of any kind at any time. The church building rattled and shook and actually began to tumble end over end until the walls were falling, collapsing around us. People were afraid and seemed to rally around me. Barriers between people were broken; we knew we needed each other.

A man named Bill Greenman was there. Bill is a personal friend who represents to me the spirit of faith. We hugged each other tightly for a long time and drew strength from each other, bonding together tremendously in the Spirit. By the time the storm finally stopped, the entire front wall of the church was gone. (Symbolically, this is what the Lord is doing in the Church today. He is knocking the front of the Church off, getting us out of the four walls.) People were confused and wanted to know what to do. Everything seemed to be in total chaos. And yet, the peace of the Lord and the Word of the Lord was resting heavily upon me. I told everyone not to worry and that we would make it out of the situation. Even as I spoke, I saw through the ruins of the church building to the outside world, which was a beautiful, scenic countryside, green with spring grass.

Before everyone had exited the church, however, I looked to the west and, in a very loud and commanding voice, declared the Word of the Lord to the Truman Sports Complex located in Kansas City, Missouri. I don't recall what I said, but I sensed judgment coming against it and even a caution for Christians not to go there lest they be found there at the wrong time and judgment come on them as well. All at once, I and the rest of the people who had been in the church seemed to be translated to Kansas City. We entered the apartment of some friends and began talking with them. However, I was unable to enter into any of the conversations because the Spirit was so heavy upon me. I sensed that something very traumatic was about to happen.

I looked out the window. That is when I felt the earthquake. Our little group rushed outside and watched as people began streaming out of the other buildings. The people were fine when they came out, but almost before I saw them I spoke out very clearly and powerfully, "The arms are coming apart! The elbow is being disjointed from the lower arm! The wrist and hand are falling apart! The knees are disjointed, and the legs and ankles are becoming separated." As I said this, it was actually happening to the people. They were literally falling apart before our eyes. In great distress and travail I cried out, "My body is a dismembered body!" The pain and anguish of the Lord was so severe that I was sobbing terribly, and yet at the same time God granted me great healing power. I would point my finger at someone's dismembered ankle, and as I focused with my eyes, it was as though laser surgery was performed from my eyes through my fingers, and healing immediately took place. This happened many times.

Then we walked down a narrow street with tall, close buildings on either side and came to a cul-de-sac. It was very run-down and neglected. As we neared the cul-de-sac, people began crying to us from within the buildings, "Is there still time for us? Will Jesus care for us too? Will He accept us?" These people were down, destitute, and full of incurable diseases.

There were drug users, addicts, people who were not in their right mind; it was like a modern-day lepers' colony. They had been confined, almost as though imprisoned, and had lost all hope. Immediately, in the power of the Spirit of the Lord, I proclaimed with great authority the Good News of the Gospel. As I began preaching, thousands poured out of the buildings and surrounded us.

Jim was with me. I knew he was praying silently. I continued to preach until suddenly all I heard was Carl Tuttle leading us in worship, singing "Lord, You Are Holy." The presence of the Lord was so strong that it seemed no one could say or sing anything else. Nothing else mattered.

When I woke up, my spirit was so stirred that I spent an hour or more crying and quietly praying to the Lord. I knew He had spoken to me and imparted something of great worth. I also recall that He warned me about people looking at God's gift or burden on a person and incorrectly perceiving that as being part of the person's personality or strength, rather than seeing that person as one of God's vessels simply carrying the Lord's cargo.

10. Two Brothers

I had this dream on January 11, 1994. In this dream, Jim and I seemed to be in Europe in a small, quaint town. There were two brothers, one sensible and one not, almost a little crazy. As time passed, because of his rigidity the sensible one began to go crazy. And the crazy one because of his freedom became sane.

11. Ronald Reagan

I was sitting by Ronald Reagan in a restaurant. He was very discouraged and was saying, "If only I could do it again." It was as if he had only served one term and had not been elected for a second. I put my head on his shoulder and said, "You can. You can." It seemed to be aimed at strength in leadership—the ability and strength to lead and overcome discouragement.

12. Bill Clinton

I dreamt that I was given the opportunity with a few other women to travel around the world with President Clinton. Someone asked me if I wanted to go. They said, "You have the money, don't you?" I looked in my wallet; I did have the money, so I decided to go. President Clinton was extremely personable and very friendly. I felt like we were making progress—that he was listening to us and becoming willing to change his ideas and policies. As we neared the end of the trip, CIA guards began to arrive, and as soon as President Clinton left our company, he reverted back to his former ways. We were discouraged because it seemed our effort and time were for nothing.

13. Headless Snakes

I saw two headless snakes that looked more like the cut-off tentacles of an octopus. These two tentacle-like headless snakes came squirming up the stairs at me. I never got hurt by them but was surprised and shocked by these headless snakes.

14. Tableland of Faith

I saw the tableland of faith. It was a large metal plate, and we were positioned around the outside of it. We were lobbing grenades over the table to the other side to protect the perimeter of it. We were trying to keep the enemy away from the boundaries. Pitching the grenades with accuracy was difficult. The enemy really wanted to come against that tableland.

15. Moses and the Masons

This is probably one of the wildest, most unusual dreams I have ever had. It was like a re-enactment of Moses' leading the Israelites to the Promised Land. At first I thought Moses was white and the Israelites were black, but I later realized that the people were very stubborn and contentious. They did not want to go and would not follow Moses' lead. When he had told them not to go in a certain direction, they had refused to listen and had gotten themselves mired in a sticky, oily, tar-like substance. They were totally covered with it, as if they had rolled around in it. Their hair was matted to their heads. They could not get it out; it would have to wear off. This was their appearance and condition throughout the whole dream.

Moses was having a terrible time trying to lead these people. They were looking for a particular kind of berry and had come to the top of a very large mountain ridge, where a sign read, "Entering Slovakia." At the time I seemed to have the understanding that they were entering Czechoslovakia. I think this was before Czechoslovakia was divided into Slovakia and the Czech Republic. As they stood at the top of this ridge, Moses saw a pinkish hue in the valley below. He tried to lead the people down the valley, knowing that they would find the fruit there. But the people didn't want to go with him, so they scattered and went in various directions. Moses went on by himself toward the fruit. When he got there he saw that these berries, which looked like raspberries, were lying about four inches thick all along the bottom and up the sides of the valley. He scooped them up in handfuls and put them in sacks.

111

Finally, the people wandered over to where Moses was and decided that they now wanted the berries. Now that Moses had gathered them, he wanted to carry them someplace. But the people tried to take them away from him and ended up fighting among themselves, ripping the bags, spilling the fruit, and making a mess of everything.

Then the scene changed to a class of young teenage boys and girls who were very contentious among themselves. This was like two different dreams that were coming in separate packages but with the same message. Two girls were doing a mock shoot-out in the classroom with play guns. They acted like it was pretend, but I saw that in their hearts they really wanted to kill each other. At one point, two teams were going to play basketball. One team was noticeably weaker and fewer in number than the other team. There were two teachers; one was good and the other was not. The good teacher decided to play on the weaker team to help even the odds. When the other teacher heard about this, he decided to join the stronger team. He wanted that team to have an unfair advantage.

There was another situation where a brother had removed a part of his sister's bicycle and hidden it in his desk. She needed to go home but couldn't unless she rode her bike. Her bicycle would not operate without the missing part. She knew where it was and asked her brother to give it to her, but he refused.

At the end of the dream all the students in the class were in a kitchen area working on various projects. Three-fourths of the students started singing a song that went something like this: "We are part of the Masons, all hail and all glory be to the rituals of the Masons. We glorify the Masons." The other fourth of the class, about four students total, turned and looked at each other in the eye. They came to a sudden realization of who they were. With the new confidence that rose up in them, they lifted up one song in unison: "All praise be to Jesus, all glory be to Jesus, we believe in Jesus." It was as if they didn't know or realize who they were until they heard the other group singing about the Masons.

III. Going Through the Doorway

I used to be so codependent on my husband. I couldn't imagine the Lord doing something special just with me. These are some of the dreams that God used to rewire me, taking out those "viruses," putting courage and vision inside of me, and letting me see myself in another light—God's light.

A. Tools for the Road

Here are a few ways to learn and gain fluency in your own dream language:

1. Get around other people who are further along than you are.

2. Get around people who dream and talk about their dreams.

3. Study different materials and various authors.

4. Get a notebook and journal your dreams.

5. Get a little recorder (15-minute tapes).

6. Get understanding.

7. Get teaching.

8. Try to set up your pre-bedtime routine so as to maximize quietness, resting, and listening. This is difficult to do, but is very helpful if you can do it.

9. Pray for impartation.

10. Love your Papa—God the Father.

Reflection Questions
Lesson Nine: Stops Along the Way

Answers to these questions can be found in the back of the study guide.

1. To gain fluency in your own dream language:

   • Get around people who _____ and talk about their _____.

   • _____ different materials, various authors.

   • _____ your dreams.

   • Use a little _____.

   • Get _____ and _____.

   • Try to set up your pre-bedtime routine so as to maximize _____, _____, and _____.

   • Pray for _____.

   • Love your _____.

2. Can you relate to any of the dreams shared in this lesson? Write out below which two dreams impacted you the most and why.

3. Write out below any insight you received when you read through the dreams that Michal Ann shared.

Journaling as a Tool for Retaining Revelation

I. Introduction

Journaling is a tried and tested biblical tool that can be used to help one retain revelation and grow in the capacity to discern the voice of the Holy Spirit. Journaling is simply a tool of keeping notes for future reference. There are various valid expressions of journaling. Journals may consist of one's prayers, what one senses to be God's answers, and/or recording what you sense the Holy Spirit is "saying" to you through His various delivery systems. It is clearly a common biblical discipline.

Some express concern that journaling is an attempt to put subjective revelation on the same level as the authority of Scripture. This is not the case. The Bible is the infallible Word of God. But in First Chronicles 28:11-19, we have an example of journaling that did not become Scripture, thus setting forth the pattern for our experience today.

God speaks to His children much of the time! However, we do not often differentiate His voice from our own thoughts, and therefore we are timid at times about stepping out in faith. If we clearly learn to retain what He is speaking to us, we will know that He has already confirmed His voice and Word to us. Thus we will be enabled to walk out God's words to us with greater confidence. Journaling then becomes a way of sorting out God's thoughts from our own.

For many, the simple discipline of recording revelation will be one of the missing links in your walk of hearing God's voice. Continuity of language, divine suggestions and reminders, and also learning the proper interpretation of symbols will occur as we use journaling as a tool for retaining revelation and discerning the voice of the Holy Spirit.

II. Lessons From Habakkuk and Daniel

A. Habakkuk 2:1-3: *"I will stand on my guard post and station myself on the rampart; and I will keep watch to see what He will speak to me, and how I may reply when I am reproved. Then the Lord answered me and said, 'Record the vision and inscribe it on tablets, that the one who reads it may run. For the vision is yet for the appointed time; it hastens towards the goal and it will not fail. Though it tarries, wait for it; for it will certainly come, it will not delay.'"*

B. Habakkuk Is Seeking a Spiritual Experience

Habakkuk is seeking to hear the *rhema* of God directly in his heart so that he can understand what he sees around him. First of all, he goes to a quiet place where he can be alone and become still. Second, he quiets himself within by watching to see what God would say. Last of all, when God begins to speak, the first thing He says is, "Record the vision." Habakkuk wrote down what he was sensing in his heart. The benefits of this journaling were retained for years to come so that those who would later read it would be able run with it.

C. Daniel 7:1: *"In the first year of Belshazzar king of Babylon Daniel saw a dream and visions in his mind as he lay on his bed; then he wrote the dream down and related the following summary of it."*

D. Daniel's Handling of Dream Revelation

If you were to read the account that follows in Daniel 7:2-14, you would note that Daniel did not write down all the details of his amazing and rather intense dream! While in a spirit of rest, he composed a summary of his encounter. Too many people get caught up in the minute details in their sincere attempts at journaling and end up missing the primary emphasis of their visitation. Be like Daniel—write down a summary and keep it simple! The Holy Spirit will have a way of bringing back to your remembrance the details that might be needed later.

III. Tips on Remembering Dreams

A. The Nature of Dreams

Some people tell me they do not hear from God in dreams—period! Others say they simply can't remember their dreams. Others seem to remember only a fragment or portions of scattered images which at the time do not seem to make a lot of sense to them.

Sleep specialists tell us though that everyone dreams for a period of time while in rapid eye movement (REM) sleep. So in reality, all of us dream at some point every night. The issue then becomes one of resting under the anointing of the Holy Spirit and recalling what we have been shown.

B. The Scriptures Speak

Job 20:8 describes what can be the fleeting nature of dreams: *"He will fly away like a dream, and not be found; yes, he will be chased away like a vision of the night"* (NKJV).

Daniel 2:1-47 also expresses the frustration that Nebuchadnezzar, king of Babylon, experienced as he received a detailed dream but could not recall it! The dream disturbed the king so much that he searched for relief and help! God heard his plea and sent Daniel, who after a season of seeking the face of God, gave him the interpretation of the dream encounter.

C. Practical Tools for Retaining Revelation

1. If possible, get rid of your loud alarm clock. Ask the Holy Spirit to help wake you up. Establish a habit of getting up at a set time, if possible.

2. Many dreams come between four to five A.M. Whenever you wake up, learn to linger in a place of rest when possible.

3. Instead of an alarm, consider waking up by using a clock radio tuned to soothing music.

D. Recording

1. Keep a note pad and pen by the bed.

2. Consider using a small tape recorder.

3. Develop your dream alphabet by keeping track of symbols.

4. Make note of your feelings/emotions in the dream/revelation.

5. Ask "What does this symbol mean to me? Can I find it in Scripture?"

6. Be still and try to recall one or two details and then your memory will kick in (see Zech. 4:2).

7. Date all entries.

8. If traveling, record the location where you had the dream.

E. Seek Training and Counsel

When possible, seek training and wise counsel from gifted interpreters of dreams. Not everyone will have this capacity as developed as others. Even in Scripture, Daniel and Joseph are the only ones who were specifically mentioned having this gift.

IV. Practical Applications in Journaling

A. Lessons in Becoming Still

1. Biblical basis (see Ps. 46:10 NKJV).

2. *First*, remove external distractions. Jesus went to a lonely place to pray (see Mark 1:35).

   Second, we must quiet our own inner being.

   a. Write down thoughts of things to do later.

   b. Release personal tensions and anxieties to the Lord (see 1 Pet. 5:7).

   c. Focus your meditating on the person of Jesus.

3. In becoming still, I am not trying to do anything. I simply want to be in touch with my Divine Lover, Jesus. I am centering on this moment of time and experiencing Him in it.

4. Remove inner noise (voices, thoughts, pressures, etc.).

B. Watching to See

In some way *rhema* is couched in vision. Habakkuk 1:1 says, *"the burden which Habakkuk the prophet saw."* He quieted himself to *watch to see* what the Lord would speak. As we have seen, focusing the eyes of our heart upon God causes us to become inwardly still; it raises our level of faith and expectancy and it makes us more fully open to receive from God.

C. Recording the Revelation

1. Find your quality time (if possible) and use it. Avoid times when you are sleepy, fatigued, or anxious.

2. A simple spiral notebook is fine. Even a tape recorder can be good.

3. This is a personal journal. Grammar, neatness, and spelling are not critical issues.

4. Date all entries.

5. Include dreams, visions, interpretations, personal feelings, and emotions as well.

6. Expect God's love toward you to be affirmed; then as you receive it, expect the gifts of the Holy Spirit to be in operation.

7. *Rhema* is tested against *logos*. Have a good knowledge of the Bible so that God can draw upon that knowledge as you record.

V. Wisdom Ways With Journaling

A. Safeguards for Your New Adventure

1. Cultivate a humble, teachable spirit. Never allow the attitude of "God told me, and that's all there is to it." All revelation is to be tested. Mistakes will be made. Accept that as part of the learning process and go on.

2. Have a good knowledge of the Bible. Remember, *rhema* is based on *logos*. The revelatory never conflicts with the written Word!

3. God primarily gives revelation for the area in which He has given responsibility and authority. A wife receives revelation about her home and children. A husband receives revelation for the home and business. A pastor will receive revelation for the church he tends. *Look for revelation in areas of your responsibility.* Stay away from ego trips that motivate you to seek revelation for areas in which God has not placed you.

4. Walk together with others. Realize that until your guidance is confirmed, it should be regarded as "what you *think* God is saying."

5. Realize that if you submit to God and resist the devil he must flee from you! (See James 4:7.) You can trust the guidance of the Holy Spirit to lead you into truth.

6. Over a period of time, you will begin to learn your spiritual alphabet, and you will mature in your understanding of the revelation you receive.

7. Add this tool of journaling to your "toolbox," and you will mature in the grace of retaining revelation and the capacity of discerning His voice.

B. Closing Prayer

Grant me the grace to journal in Jesus' great name. Teach me the skills of how to retain revelation and clearly discern the flow of Your voice. Lead me in Your wisdom applications of recording what You reveal. In Jesus' name, Amen.

Reflection Questions
Lesson Ten: Journaling as a Tool for Retaining Revelation

Answers to these questions can be found in the back of the study guide.

1. Journaling then becomes a way of sorting out _____ thoughts from _____ thoughts.

2. When you journal, write down a _____ and keep it _____. The Holy Spirit will have a way of bringing back to your remembrance the _____ that might be needed later.

3. Sleep specialists tell us that _____ percent of us dream at some point every night.

4. List below any ways that you are presently recording the revelation that God gives to you. From Section III C and D or Section IV, what are a few additional ways God is leading you to retain and record the revelation that He gives to you?

5. Psalm 46:10 (NKJV) says, "_____ _____ *and know that I am God.*"

6. Cultivate a _____, _____ spirit. All revelation is to be tested, and _____ will be made. Accept that as part of the learning process and go on.

7. God primarily gives revelation for the area in which He has given you _____ and _____.

8. Walk together with _____.

9. *Rhema* is based on *logos*. What does this mean?

10. Write down the primary insight you gained from this lesson and how God is leading you to apply it to your life.

LESSON ELEVEN

When God Seems Silent

I. He Did Not Answer With a Word

"Wet seasons" are times of blessing, of growth and expansion, of fruitfulness and promotion. "Dry seasons" are seasons of pruning and preparation in anticipation of the next wet season. Dry seasons are the times of the cross and wet seasons are the times of resurrection life. In order to build healthy, balanced Christian lives we need both.

A. Personal Background

1. Youth Choir Loft Experience

I was a singer from a young age, often positioned in the loft, patiently looking down on the congregation as the pianist, organist, and pastor on the platform would perform opening rituals. Many times I was the one who began the service. Standing in the darkened loft alone with no instrument, I would sing, "The Lord is in His holy temple; let all the earth keep silent before Him." And then the service would proceed. I sang that Sunday after Sunday until my voice began to change. I still remember the Sunday I quit. I sang high and then suddenly low in one phrase. I was so embarrassed that I did not come down from the balcony but stayed up in the loft. That Sunday I received one of my first lessons in silence.

2. No Words for Me

When I entered into a traveling ministry years later, I traveled all over North America and visited several other countries, releasing prophetic words to people everywhere I went. I spoke thousands of prophetic words of encouragement to individuals, congregations, leaders, cities, and nations. Yet during all those years of releasing public prophetic words to others, I rarely, if ever, received a public prophetic word myself. It was especially painful that all my ministerial buddies were getting three and four prophetic words, public affirmations, direction, etc.—and I was not. I did not understand it. God seemed silent.

3. Times of the Dark Night of the Soul

God does speak. He has spoken to us many times in the past, and He will continue to speak to us in the future. But many times as a family it has seemed as though God was silent. Where was His miracle work? Where was His hedge of protection? Where was the God of supernatural encounters? Where was God when I needed Him? We have experienced days, weeks, yes, *months*, when God seemed silent.

The word *seemed* is very important here. God may seem silent at times, but He is always active. God is always at work. Yet He does not always tell us what He is doing at the time. All we can do is recall His past faithfulness in speaking to us and trust that He will do so again according to His own timetable.

B. Matthew 15:21-24—Lessons From a Desperate Mother

"Jesus…withdrew into the district of Tyre and Sidon. And a Canaanite woman from that region came out and began to cry out, saying, 'Have mercy on me, Lord, Son of David; my daughter is cruelly demon-possessed.' But He did not answer her a word. And His disciples came and implored Him, saying, 'Send her away, because she keeps shouting at us.' But He answered and said, 'I was sent only to the lost sheep of the house of Israel.'"

1. Jesus withdrew from Jerusalem to Tyre and Sidon.

2. A Canaanite woman came out to meet him.

3. She lifted a cry for "mercy" for her demonized daughter.

4 Jesus did not answer her a word.

5.   The disciples said, "Send her away—she's obnoxious!"

6.   Jesus said, "I came to the Lost House of Israel."

II. How Do We Respond?

A. Handling the "Why" Question

"A man can live with his existence if he has a 'why' for his existence."

You can make it through almost anything if you know why. The day came when even Jesus Himself had a dry season. Throughout eternity, the Son of God had enjoyed unbroken fellowship with His Father. Never had Jesus known the silence of His Father—until He went to the cross. As all the sin of the human race from every generation came crashing down on Jesus' shoulders at Calvary, He felt His Father turn His face away. In anguish He cried out, *"My God, My God, why have You forsaken Me?"* (Matt. 27:46b). As far as we know from Scripture, Jesus never received an answer. The One who allows us to experience dry seasons knows exactly how it feels to go through such a time. I draw comfort and encouragement from this. Jesus knows how we feel when God seems silent, and He can help us get through it.

B. Jesus Was Given Fully to the Issue of "Why"

"Why have You forsaken Me?" are the words of Jesus on the cross.

III. Handling the "How & When" Questions

A. John 5:1-9—Lessons from the Pool of Bethsaida

"After these things there was a feast of the Jews, and Jesus went up to Jerusalem. Now there is in Jerusalem by the sheep gate a pool, which is called in Hebrew Bethesda, having five porticoes. In these lay a multitude of those who were sick, blind, lame, and withered, [waiting for the moving of the waters; for an angel of the Lord went down at certain seasons into the pool and stirred up the water; whoever then first, after the stirring up of the water, stepped in was made well from whatever disease with which he was afflicted.] A man was there who had been ill for thirty-eight years. When Jesus saw him lying there, and knew that he had already been a long time in that condition, He said to him, 'Do you wish to get well?' The sick man answered Him, 'Sir, I have no man to put me into the pool

when the water is stirred up, but while I am coming, another steps down before me.' Jesus said to him, 'Get up, pick up your pallet and walk.' Immediately the man became well, and picked up his pallet and began to walk....Now it was the Sabbath on that day."

1. The man was sick for 38 years.

2. He was lying by the pool—waiting.

3. The first one in the waters after they were stirred was healed.

4. Multitudes in desperation were there!

5. The man asked, "How do I get in? When will the angel come?"

6. Jesus came and asked a question: "Do you want to get well?"

7. The man's response comes from the fatigue factor of delay—"I have no one to help me into the pool."

B. When Others Got in and Were Healed...

1. When others were healed, did he (you) rejoice?

2. What did that do to your faith?

3. He didn't get himself there. He couldn't get himself out. He couldn't get into the pool.

C. When the Waters Are Stirred and Nothing Happens

1. Look past the outward...look into the heart.

2. Why are you (they) still here?

3. The unshakable Kingdom is being established.

D. When the Enemy Comes...

1. "You don't deserve revelation!"

2. "God doesn't want to endorse you!"

3. "Does God know where I live?"

4. "Forget you guys! Hang it up!"

IV. Perspective in the Midst of the Valley

A. Why Isn't God Speaking? Why Is There a Withholding of Revelation?

Years ago in Kansas City, I had the privilege of being exposed to realms of the prophetic that were absolutely profound. The top seers, statesmen, dreamers, prophetic teachers, and prophetic intercessors were all in a strange collegiality together. People came from all over the world to see who we were. I was younger and gifted and less secure in my identity in Christ. As I shared earlier, I did not get the confirmation that I thought I deserved and needed. I began asking the "why," "how," and "when" questions. From my perspective, compared to all those I was walking with at that time, God seemed silent. As I searched out these questions, I realized the following:

1. I was relying too much on an external witness.

2. It was not the *kairos* moment yet. Strategic timing had not yet come.

3. My expectations were misplaced, too high, or off base.

4. I was chasing for words from men and not the Word itself. Human words fail, but God's Word never fails.

5. There were spiritual warfare attacks—deaf and dumb spirits hindering mine and others' ability to hear, speak, release, and receive.

B. Responses to Dry Seasons

Frustrated over the whole business, I remember saying, "Lord, I don't need to play this game any more. You are my source!" Did I still care? Yes. Did I still have needs? Yes. But I was finished with chasing men for words. And that is when things began to change.

1. Stick with what we already know—what was the last thing the Lord said?

2. You might be in a test—what do you believe?

3. Don't doubt in darkness what you have seen or heard in times of light.

4. Don't compare yourself to others!

5. Be childlike...don't be overly complicated!

6. Don't expect everything to be so dramatic! Don't be a prophetic junky!

7. How about the person sitting next to you?

8. Walk by faith—not by sight.

9. Learn the lessons of guidance.

V. **God's Purposes in Times of Silence**

A. **Matthew 15:25-28—How to Respond When Offended!**

"But she came and began to bow down before Him, saying, 'Lord, help me!' And He answered and said, 'It is not good to take the children's bread and throw it to the dogs.' But she said, 'Yes, Lord; but even the dogs feed on the crumbs which fall from their masters' table.' Then Jesus said to her, 'O woman, your faith is great; it shall be done for you as you wish.' And her daughter was healed at once."

1. Bow low. Worship.

2. Receive a revelation of dependency—"Lord, have mercy on me!"

3. Keep your heart clean—more opportunities for offenses will come!

4. God offends the mind to reveal the heart.

5. Be tenacious! Do not let go.

6. Receive your inheritance!

7. Rejoice and know your victory is another person's test.

B. **God Is on the Other Side!**

Your dry season is God's way of building character and preparing you for bigger and greater things. He has promised that He will never leave you or forsake you. When God seems silent, believe that He guides you even from His silence.

1. Believe He guides:

    ▪   He has guided me in the past!

- He is guiding me now!
- He will guide me in the future!

2. Be sensitive to others. Create within yourself a capacity for compassion.

3. God is more than a jukebox machine ready to play your favorite tune.

4. Learn how to hear God for yourself.

5. Trust Him! You have a Father!

6. Identify with Jesus on the cross.

7. Silence is an invitation to greater union with Christ!

Reflection Questions
Lesson Eleven: When God Seems Silent

Answers to these questions can be found in the back of the study guide.

1. Take a moment and reflect upon your most recent dry season or dark night of the soul—possibly one that you are in presently. Write out below some of the lies the enemy sent (or is sending) your way.

2. Write out below how you have handled the "why," "how," and "when" questions and any insight you have received during this season.

3. Ask the Holy Spirit right now to show you if you have fallen into any of the five points below taken from Section IV A.   Circle any that apply to you.

   • Relying too much on an external witness.

   • Strategic timing has not yet come.

   • Expectations are misplaced, too high, or off base.

   • Chasing for words from men and not the Word Himself.

   • Spiritual warfare attacks.

4. From Section IV B, review the responses to a dry season. Write out two below that you believe God is highlighting for you.

   _____

   _____

5. From Section V, A and B, review God's purposes in times of silence. Write out three below that you believe God is highlighting for you. Spend a moment in

prayer asking the Lord to help you see each of these and the issues from question 3 from His point of view. Tell Him how you want to respond in dry seasons and ask that your roots would grow deeper when water is scarce.

_____

_____

_____

6. When God seems silent, believe that He _____ you even from His silence.

Handling Dreams With Wisdom

I. The Necessity of the Wisdom Ways of God

A. Revelation Is "Hot Stuff"

Watch out! Dreams and revelation can be hot stuff! You can be burned by it if you mishandle it. It is like a pot of boiling water on a stove. Put on the mittens of wisdom to carry the cargo to its place of usefulness and purpose. Otherwise, it might spill on you!

B. After Revelation Comes

After revelation, we must call forth God's wisdom administration. It we do not, through mismanagement of the dream, it can burn rather than heal and empower. Remember Proverbs 12:8: *"A man will be praised according to his insight."* Ask for His insight with wisdom and understanding—the Lord will grant it.

C. Some Possible Applications for Beginners

1. When interpreting a dream and presenting it to others, **turn your thoughts into a question:** "Does this indicate anything for me to do?"

2. **Turn your dreams into intercession.** Pray the inspiration instead of sweating out bullets of heavy perspiration!

3. **Submit your revelation to trusted counsel (and even a council).** God will not give all of it to you. Trust Him to speak through others as well.

4. **If you've received the genuine article, there is tension to know what to do** with what you receive. Do you sit on this, or run with it? This tension is normal and part of your learning curve.

5. Eventually, **another test will come.** You will be praised (elevated) because of your (really His) gift. What will you do with these trophies? Bob Mumford years ago said, "At the end of the day, I present my trophies to the Lord, and I worship Him with them."

6. Learn the lesson quickly and well from Proverbs 29:11 (paraphrased): "A fool opens wide his mouth and tells all he knows." Ask the Holy Spirit questions. Watch and learn from others. What do I say? To whom do I give it? When do I release it? Where do I present it? Most of us learn this proverb by mistake and the tutor of experience!

D. **Second-Heaven Revelation**

Different groups and individuals use different terms for this. Not everything you receive is a declaration of what is supposed to come to pass. It is possible that the Holy Spirit could give you insight into one of satan's schemes or plans (Paul said we are not to be ignorant of the devil's schemes).

Thus second-heaven revelation is sometimes referred to as that information that derives from the enemy's camp and is used to enlighten us so as to prepare us or stop it from occurring.

E. **Give Your Revelation With Gentleness**

Try brokenness. Hard confrontation is the exception, not the norm. Go through the standard procedures of first speaking, second exhorting, and third warning with all authority. This is according to the pattern of Titus 2:8 (also see Gal. 6:1; 2 Tim. 2:23-26).

F. **Wisdom Shouts the Fear of the Lord**

See Proverbs 9:10. Do not use your revelation as a tool of punishment. The Holy Spirit spoke to me once, "Be careful not to stretch the rod of your mouth out against the house that the Lord builds."

G. Beware: You Can Become Tainted by an Evil Report

You can become tainted by an evil report given to you by a person about someone else under the guise of revelation. Numbers 13 and 14 are important chapters for us to read and learn today! Get washed in the blood of Jesus from the defilement of gossip and evil reports.

H. Be Alert to the Activity of the "Accuser of the Brethren"

He tries to spew filthy inspiration on believers (see Rev. 12:10; Prov. 10:18). Be alert. The devil prowls around like a roaring lion seeking someone he may devour (see 1 Pet. 5:8).

Bart Druckenmiller in his book *Dreams in the Spirit* says it this way, "It is very easy to misinterpret people's actions, motives, or intentions as well as all types of things, especially in dreams. You may find yourself having a dream about a character flaw in someone else's life and think the problem is with them, when God is really trying to show you something in your own life.

"Here is an important principle in dream interpretation: if the dream contradicts what you already know to be true, hold on to what you know to be true, and not [your understanding] of the dream. We must quit shooting our wounded, which is what the accuser does. We don't need to help him."[1]

II. How to Respond to Your Dreams

Always remember the simple three-stage process when handling revelation of all types: revelation, interpretation, and application. If you miss it in step two, step three (application) is doomed to failure! So seek God's Word, His will, and His ways when handling dreams.

A. Simple Steps to Take!

The following are some simple steps for us to consider in responding to our dreams.

- Allow peace to rule in your mind and heart at all times.

- Write out a summary of the dream and date it.

- Pray over the events and circumstances of the dream—its content *and* how it came to you.

- At times seek wise confidential counsel on how to proceed.

- Consider seeking interpretation through others who are not involved in the situation.

- Do not act on the dream until the interpretation is confirmed. Seek confirmation at all times. Remember, God always confirms His Word by more than one witness.

- When the dream's meaning has been confirmed, only take first steps toward the fulfillment of it. This is particularly true when dealing with dreams concerning your calling.

- Always remember that dreams are what your prophetic potential is— not automatic declarations of what will be!

- Dreams almost always lead to a process of becoming. Dr. Joe Ibojie in his book *Dreams and Visions* aptly states, "An appropriate interpretation should bring you closer to God. The journey is as important as the destination to God. He measures maturity and character, but the dreamer may be more time conscious of progress as a measure of time. The process took Joseph 17 years to fulfill, but it was worth the waiting."[2]

- A dream may not always be logical! But hang on to it and treasure it in your heart.

- Plant the dreams in your heart and spirit and always remember—if they are from God they are worth a good fight! Wage war with the promise when the circumstances seem to run contrary to the dream. Do not give up on your dreams!

B. Testing Dreams

1. Does the dream seem to contradict God's nature of being a good and loving Father who desires the best for each of His kids?

2. Does the dream contradict the principles of the written Word of God?

3. Does the dream glorify Jesus Christ and point people to Him and the work of His cross?

4. Does the dream build up your faith and cause you to desire a closer walk with the Lover of your soul?

5. Does the dream produce freedom in the grace of God or does it bring you and others into bondage and legalism?

6. Does the dream line up with God's overall plan for your life and seem to be a progression of what has already been revealed?

7. Does the dream cause you to move towards fellowship with the Body of Christ or does it create alienation and disorientation?

III. The Wisdom Model From Daniel's Life[3]

The necessity of wisdom-filled and God-guided dream interpreters is great today. But as the end of the age unfolds, ambassadors of revelation with humble and accurate presentation will be needed all the more. Therefore, let's seek the Lord for a Daniel-type model to be restored.

The Book of Daniel provides an excellent pattern for us to follow. The following outline paraphrases Chuck Pierce's book *When God Speaks*. The following shows Nebuchadnezzar's dreams and the process through which Daniel interpreted them.

A. Daniel Determined the Source of the Dreams

Daniel determined this was his assignment in God and that there was a revelatory message from God in dreams that he was to find. This is always the first critical step. Determine the source!

B. Daniel Asked for Time to Interpret the Dream

According to Daniel 2:16 *"Daniel went in and requested of the king that he would give him time, in order that he might declare the interpretation to the king."* We are the recipients of divine wisdom. No one has it except Spirit-filled believers in Jesus! Seek the Lord and seek His godly counselors. First Corinthians 2:6 says it this way, *"Yet we do speak wisdom among those who are mature; a wisdom, however, not of this age nor of the rulers of this age, who are passing away."*

C. Daniel Rallied People to Pray

Daniel 2:17-18 states, *"Then Daniel went to his house and informed his friends, Hananiah, Mishael and Azariah, about the matter, so that they might request compassion from the God of heaven concerning this mystery, so that Daniel and his friends would not be destroyed with the rest of the wise men of Babylon."* Intercession always pays off!

D. Daniel Received Revelation from the Lord

Daniel 2:19 tells us *"the mystery was revealed to Daniel in a night vision."* Only God can do such a thing! Mysteries invite intrigue, but only God can release the meaning.

E. Daniel Worshiped His God

Daniel 2:20-23: *"Let the name of God be blessed forever and ever, for wisdom and power belong to Him. It is He who changes the times and the epochs; He removes kings and establishes kings; He gives wisdom to wise men and knowledge to men of understanding. It is He who reveals the profound and hidden things; He knows what is in the darkness, and the light dwells with Him. To You, O God of my fathers, I give thanks and praise, for You have given me wisdom and power; even now You have made known to me what we requested of You, for You have made known to us the king's matter."*

This is a major key in Daniel's life—he was a worshiper! No wonder the Holy Spirit liked hanging out with Daniel! He worshiped the Lord as His source of revelation and wisdom.

F. Daniel Wisely Interpreted the Dream

Daniel 2:36-45 gives the interpretation of the king's dream. Like Daniel, when interpreting a dream for someone else, we need to be sensitive in our approach as to how to interpret and deliver the message we have received.

IV. A Voice That Can Be Heard

A. At times there is a struggle and a tension we have to deal with in order to properly handle even the correct interpretation of dreams and revelation. Suppose more than one person receives similar or even the exact same content. Both individuals then present their truths to those intended. Why is one person received and recognized and another is not? Why is it that one person appears to be valued and others are not? What constitutes a voice that can be heard?

Let's consider the following possibilities in this maze of complexity.

1. It is the strategic purpose and timing of God for one and not necessarily for the other to be promoted.

2. For one it is a season of favor—for the other it is a season of character formation and preparation.

3. There is a strategic joining relationally that is to occur with the dreamer and/or interpreter and the recipient of the revelation.

4. One has a sphere that includes a higher public profile—another's sphere is the intercessor's closet.

5. For one it is divine protection—for the other it is graduation.

6. For one there has been an accumulation of investment—for another it is their first or second interaction with that sphere.

7. For one there is a relational bridge of trust—with the others—the bridge has been damaged or remains untested.

8. While the content might be the same—the manner of delivery is not. The leader/recipient always has the choice of which style they wish to have promoted publicly in their house, church, and sphere of authority.

9. Some things remain a mystery! We are never exempt from trusting in the Lord with all our heart and not leaning on our own understanding. It is His business! Let God be God! Learn to thank Him that you have been used as a voice of confirmation. Let Him be your affirmation!

V. Presenting a Dream to a King

Want to give a word to a king? Want to be used to interpret a king's dream? Want to be brought before people of influence? How would you carry a message to such a person? With these principles in mind, consider the following thoughts.

- **Character to Carry the Gift!**

   The issues of integrity and honor are of utmost importance when approaching a king or person of influence! Humility, internal security, and trust in God are essential! When studying the lives of Daniel, Joseph, Esther, and others, you will find that the way of approach can be as important as the message brought. Being a voice that can be heard deals as much with prophetic protocol as it does with content! Yet, walking in the fear of the Lord versus the fear of man is also critical!

- **Each Believer in Christ Jesus is a Priest and a King!**

   Revelation 1:5b and 6 declares, *"To Him who loves us and released us from our sins by His blood—and He has made us to be a kingdom, priests to His God and Father—to Him be the glory and the dominion forever and ever. Amen."* If this be the case, then when approaching any of God's children, we should also do it with integrity, honor, and humility. Realize—each us are kings in God's eyes!

- **God Is Our Ultimate King!**

   Want to give God a word? How does a priestly watchman give his commander and chief a word? Yes, use the same heart qualities of honor and humility mixed with boldness as you approach the gracious courts of the King. Prophetic intercession is the means of giving the King of the universe a word of consultation, or an appeal for intervention and direction. Join others and me in the amazing art of intervention by presenting your dreams before the King of kings!

VI. Things to Always Do With Dreams!

A. Earnestly Desire the Gifts of the Holy Spirit

Especially desire that you may prophesy (see 1 Cor. 14:1).

Not only does God want to speak to you, but He also wants to speak *through* you! Be a dreamer for God's sake! Volunteer!

B. Believe God's Prophets and You'll Succeed

Second Chronicles 20:20 gives us 20/20 vision. Rejoice! What a privilege you have been given. Mix faith with God's words and receive the Lord's results. But place your faith in the God of the Word, not in the man of the word.

C. Pray the Promise Back to God

Follow Daniel's example of reminding God of His Word through intercession (see Jer. 29:10; Dan. 9:1-19). Bathe the dream experience in prayer. (For further study see my book *Kneeling on the Promises* by Chosen Books.)

D. Fight the Good Fight!

Use the word revealed through a dream as equipment for spiritual battle (see 1 Tim. 1:18). Do spiritual warfare against discouragement, doubt, unbelief, and fear through declaring and reciting what the prophetic dream states concerning you.

E. Seek Confirmation at All Times

Remember, out of the mouth of two or three witnesses every fact is to be confirmed and established (see Deut. 19:15; Matt. 18:16; 2 Cor. 13:1).

F. Dare to Believe and Then Obey!

Are you a believing believer? Are you listening and then obeying? Herman Riffel in his book *Learning to Hear God's Voice* states, "Obedience is the expression of faith and the key to learning to recognize God's voice ever more clearly. We need to be willing to risk those little mistakes as we venture in faith, and trust God to protect us from the big ones."[4]

VII. Conclusion

Go on a great adventure with Michal Ann and me! Receive the spirit of revelation and be a dreamer! Step out on the limb of faith and do something for Jesus' sake! Remember—God is the one who promised to pour out His Spirit on all flesh in the time of the last days. It is His will to give dreams and visions and revelation (see Joel 2:28 and Acts 2:17-18). Believe! Receive and obey the Word of the Lord! Dreams are our last days' inheritance!

Endnotes

1. Bart Druckenmiller, *Dreams in the Spirit* (Shippensburg, PA: Treasure House, 1999).

2. Joe Ibojie, *Dreams and Visions: How to Receive, Interpret, and Apply Your Dreams* (Pescara, Italy: Destiny Image Europe, 2005).

3. The outline for the discussion of Daniel in this section is adapted from Chuck Pierce and Rebecca Wagner Sytsema, *When God Speaks: How to Interpret Dreams, Visions, Signs and Wonders* (Ventura, CA: Gospel Light, 2005), 81-83.

4. Herman Riffel, *Learning to Hear God's Voice* (Old Tappan, NJ: Chosen Books, 1986), 144-145.

Reflection Questions
Lesson Twelve: Handling Dreams With Wisdom

Answers to these questions can be found in the back of the study guide.

1. After revelation, we must call forth God's _____ _____.

2. What are six applications for handling dreams as a beginner?

   _____

   _____

   _____

   _____

   _____

   _____

3. "Second-heaven revelation" is information used to enlighten us so as to _____ us or _____ it from occurring.

4. Hard _____ is the exception, not the norm. God wants us to give revelation with _____.

5. From Section III, review the six principles of the wisdom model from Daniel's life. List two below that you feel the Lord is highlighting for you to remember.

   _____

   _____

6. From Section IV, review the nine considerations of your voice as "a voice that can be heard." List a few below that especially apply to you. Ask the Lord for discernment as you reflect on your own experiences.

7. The issues of _____ and _____ are of utmost importance when approaching a king or person of influence.

8. Six key things to remember to always do with dreams are

   • Earnestly desire the _____ of the Holy Spirit.

- Believe God's _____, and you'll succeed.

- Pray the _____ back to God.

- _____ the good fight!

- Seek _____ at all times.

- Dare to _____ and then _____!

Concluding Exercise:

1. Review the Reflection Questions from each of the twelve lessons. Ask the Lord to show you one point that He wants you to take away from each lesson. Highlight it in some way on the page (i.e., circle it, use a highlighter).

2. When you are done with Exercise 1, summarize each of the twelve points in the space provided below. Then take some time to pray through the list. Ask the Lord how He wants you to apply them to your life. Circle those that God is leading you to act on immediately. Also write out any specific ways the Holy Spirit leads you to implement what He has spoken to you and take bold steps of faith in that direction.

1)

2)

3)

4)

5)

6)

7)

8)

9)

10)

11)

12)

Answers to the Reflection Questions

Lesson One

1. skeptical; sophisticated; heritage

2. a series of thoughts, images, or emotions that appear in our minds during sleep

3. whet; hungry

4. hindrances

5. same; today

6. receiver

7. **Unbelievers:** Abimelech, Laban, Pharaoh's butler and baker, Pharaoh, Midian, Nebuchadnezzar, wise men, Pilate's wife. **Believers:** Abraham, Jacob, Daniel, Joseph, Solomon, Joseph, Paul.

8. personal God; natural man; demonic darkness

Lesson Two

4. John 5:19-20; Romans 6:13-16; Ephesians 1:17-19; 2 Kings 6:17; Genesis 40:8

Lesson Three

1. 1) Who is this person in relation to you? 2) What does the person's name mean? 3) What character trait or calling do they represent to you?

4. wisdom; discernment; prayer

5. dictionary and the Bible; journaling; anointing, gifts, and presence of the Holy Spirit

Lesson Four

1. enemy; snatch; revelation

2. submit; resist; flee

3. traditions; theology, worldview; Hebraic; Greek

4. integrity; call; authority

5. distraction; disinformation; disbelief; the downward spiral

6. pulling out your spiritual antenna; the power of the blood; praying in the Spirit; meditation in the Word; worship

Lesson Five

1. generational

2. redemptive

3. relationships; relationship

4. free

5. viruses

6. eggs

7. freedom from distractions; barriers are down

8. Leads you to the heart of the Father; awakens your walk with God; imparts intercessory burdens; launches you into ministry; brings healing

9. It drives you deeper to discover what it means—what God is saying to you.

Lesson Six

1. diverse, creative, love

2. revelation

3. truth

4. sphere; influence

5. faith; gift; authority

6. dreams of self disclosure (sometimes called internal or intrinsic); help; dreams of outside events (sometimes called external or extrinsic); intercession

8. simple

9. message; symbolic; complex symbolic

Lesson Seven

1. Helper

2. Counselor; Teacher; Tutor

3. ask

Lesson Eight

1. again

2. symbolism; parables

3. Scripture; colloquial expressions; personal revelatory alphabet

4. visual; actual

5. simplest

8. We may well despise the realization of the dream when it finally arrives. It can also steal our joy and blind us to the dream for which we have longed.

Lesson Nine

1. dream; dreams; Study; Journal; recorder; understanding; teaching; quietness, resting, listening; impartation; Papa

Lesson Ten

1. God's; our

2. summary; simple; details

3. 100

4. See Section III C and D for specific options

5. Be still

6. humble; teachable; mistakes

7. responsibility; authority

8. others

9. The revelatory (*rhema*) never conflicts with the written Word (*logos*).

Lesson Eleven

6. guides

Lesson Twelve

1. wisdom administration

2. Turn your thoughts into a question; turn your dream into intercession; submit your revelation to trusted counsel; know that if you've received the genuine article, there is a tension to know what to do with what you receive; another test will come—present your "trophies" to the Lord and worship Him with them; learn the lesson quickly and well from Proverbs 29:11 (paraphrased), *"A fool opens wide his mouth and tells all he knows."*

3. prepare; stop

4. confrontation; gentleness

7. integrity; honor

8. gifts; prophets; promise; fight; confirmation; believe, obey

Recommended Reading

Addison, Doug. *Prophecy, Dreams, and Evangelism*. North Sutton, NH: Streams Publishing House, 2005.

Bullinger, Ethelbert W. *Number in Scripture*. Grand Rapids, MI: Kregel Publications, 1967.

Conner, Kevin. *Interpreting the Symbols and Types*. Portland, OR: Bible Temple Publications, 1992.

Goll, James W. *The Beginner's Guide to Hearing God*. Ventura, CA: Regal Books, 2004.

___. *The Coming Prophetic Revolution*. Grand Rapids, MI: Chosen Books, 2001.

___. *Consecrated Contemplative Prayer*. Franklin, TN: Encounters Network, 2005.

___. *Experiencing Dreams and Visions Study Guide*. Franklin, TN: Encounters Network, 2005.

___. *The Lost Art of Practicing His Presence*. Shippensburg, PA: Destiny Image, 2006.

___. *The Seer*. Shippensburg, PA: Destiny Image Publishers, 2004.

___. *Understanding Supernatural Encounters Study Guide*. Franklin, TN: Encounters Network, 2005.

Goll, James W. and Michal Ann Goll, *God Encounters*. Shippensburg, PA: Destiny Image Publishers, 2005.

___. *Dream Language*, Shippensburg, PA: Destiny Image, 2006.

Goll, Michal Ann. *Women on the Front Line*. Shippensburg, PA: Destiny Image, 1999.

Hamon, Jane. *Dreams and Visions*. Ventura, CA: Regal Books, 2000.

Ibojie, Dr. Joe. *Dreams and Visions: How to Receive, Interpret, and Apply Your Dreams*. Pescara, Italy: Destiny Image Europe, 2005.

Kelsey, Morton. *God, Dreams, and Revelation*. Minneapolis, MN: Augsburg Publishers, 1991.

Milligan, Ira. *Understanding the Dreams You Dream*. Shippensburg, PA: Destiny Image, 1997.

Ochs, Vanessa L. and Elizabeth Ochs. *The Jewish Dream Book*. Woodstock, VT: Jewish Lights Publishing, 2003.

Pierce, Chuck and Rebecca Sytsema. *When God Speaks*. Ventura, CA: Gospel Light, 2005.

Randolph, Larry. *Spirit Talk*. Wilkesboro, NC: Morningstar Publications, 2005.

Riffel, Herman. *Dream Interpretation*. Shippensburg, PA: Destiny Image, 1993.

Rutland, Mark. *Dream*. Lake Mary, FL: Charisma House, 2003.

Sandford, John, and Paula. *The Elijah Task*. Plainfield, NJ: Logos International, 1977.

Thomas, Benny. *Exploring the World of Dreams*. Springdale, PA: Whitaker House, 1990.

Tompkins, Iverna, with Judson Cornwall. *On the Ash Heap With No Answers*. Lake Mary, FL: Creation House, 1992.

Virkler, Mark, and Patti. *Communion With God*. Shippensburg, PA: Destiny Image, 1990.

Wilkinson, Bruce. *The Dream Giver*. Sisters, OR: Multnomah Publishers, Inc., 2003.

Wilson, Walter. *Wilson's Dictionary of Bible Types*. Grand Rapids, MI: William B. Eerdmans Publishing Company, 1957.

Index of Dream Symbols and Types

Acid Bitter, offense, carrying a grudge, hatred, sarcasm

Alligator Ancient, evil out of the past (through inherited or personal sin), danger, destruction, evil spirit

Altar A symbol for sacrifice and for incense

Anchor Representation of safety and hope

Arm Represents God's power and strength

Armor A symbol of warfare

Ashes Memories, repentance, ruin, destruction

Automobile Life, person, ministry

Autumn End, completion, change, repentance

Axe Represents warfare and judgment

Baby New beginning, new idea, dependent, helpless, innocent, sin

Balance(s) Represents judgment

Barn Symbol for blessings

Bat Witchcraft, unstable, flighty, fear

Beard Represents old age and wisdom

Beaver Industrious, busy, diligent, clever, ingenious

Bed Rest, salvation, meditation, intimacy, peace, covenant (marriage, natural or evil), self-made

Bicycle Works, works of the flesh, legalism, self-righteousness, working out life's difficulties, messenger

Bird Symbol of spirits, good or evil, (see the parable of Jesus on the birds)

Black Symbol of famine and death

Blood Symbol for sacrifice and for life (life is in the blood)

Blue Symbol of Heaven

Bow Usually represents judgment

Bread Represents life

Brick Represents slavery and human effort

Bridle Symbol of restraint, control

Brother-in-Law Partiality or adversary, fellow minister, problem relationship, partner, oneself, natural brother-in-law

Brown Dead (as in plant life), repentant, born again, without spirit

Bull Persecution, spiritual warfare, opposition, accusation, slander, threat, economic increase

Butterfly Freedom, flighty, fragile, temporary glory

Camel Represents servanthood, bearing the burden of others

Candle Symbol of light (Holy Spirit or the spirit of man)

Candlestick Represents the Church

Cat Self-willed, untrainable, predator, unclean spirit, bewitching charm, stealthy, sneaky, deception, self-pity, something precious in the context of a personal pet

Caterpillar Represents judgment and destructive powers

Censer Symbol of intercession and worship

Chain Symbol of binding, oppression, punishment

Chicken Fear, cowardliness; hen can be protection, gossip, motherhood; rooster can be boasting, bragging, proud; chick can be defenseless, innocent

Circle Symbol of eternity

City Symbol of security, safety, permanency (cities of refuge)

Cloud and Fiery Pillar Represents divine presence, covering, and guidance

Colt Represents bearing burden of others or could be a portrayal of stubbornness

Corn (oil and wine) Represents blessings of God

Crow (raven) Confusion, outspoken, operating in envy or strife, hateful, direct path, unclean, God's minister of justice or provision

Cup Symbol of life, health, or could represent death and evil

Cymbal Symbol of vibration, praise, worship

Deer Graceful, swift, sure-footed, agile, timid

Desert Desolation, temptation, solitude

Dog Unbelievers, religious hypocrites

Door An opening, entrance

Dove Holy Spirit

Dragon satan

Dreaming A message within a message, aspiration, vision

Drowning Overcome, self-pity, depression, grief, sorrow, temptation, excessive debt

Drugs Influence, spell, sorcery, witchcraft, control, legalism, medicine, healing

Eight New beginnings

Eight-Eight-Eight The first resurrection saints

Elephant Invincible or thick-skinned, not easily offended, powerful, large

Elevator Changing position, going into the spirit realm, elevated, demoted

Eleven Incompleteness, disorder

Eye(s) Omniscience, knowledge, sight, insight, foresight

Face Character, countenance

Falling Unsupported, loss of support (financial, moral, public), trial, succumb, backsliding

Father Authority, God, author, originator, source, inheritance, tradition, custom, satan, natural father

Father-in-Law Law, authoritative relationship based on law, legalism, problem authoritative relationship, natural father-in-law

Feathers Covering, protection

Feet Heart, walk, way, thoughts (meditation), offense, stubborn (unmovable), rebellion (kicking), sin

Fifty Symbol of liberty, freedom, Pentecost

Fig Relates to Israel as a nation

Fig Leaves Self-atonement, self-made covering

Finger Feeling, sensitivity, discernment, conviction, works, accusation (as in pointing a finger), instruction

Fire Presence of God, holiness of God, purifying, testing

Fish Souls of men

Five God's grace to man, responsibility of man

Flies Evil spirits, filth of satan's kingdom; beelzebub—"lord of flies"

Flood Judgment on sin and violence (the flood from Noah's time)

Flower Fading glory of man

Forest Symbol of nations

Fortress Protection, a stronghold

Forty Symbol of testing, trial, closing in victory or defeat (Israel in the wilderness and Jesus in the desert)

Forty-Five Preservation

Forty-Two Israel's oppression, the Lord's advent to the earth

Fountain Source of life, refreshing

Four Represents worldwide, universal (as in four corners of the earth)

Fourteen Passover, time of testing

Fox Cunning, evil men

Friend Self, the character or circumstance of one's friend reveals something about oneself; sometimes one friend represents another (look for the same name, initials, hair color); sometimes represents actual friend

Frog Demons, unclean spirits

Garden Growth and fertility

Gate A way of entrance, power, authority

Gold Kingship, Kingdom glory, God or gods

Grandchild Heir, oneself, inherited blessing or iniquity, one's spiritual legacy, actual grandchild

Grandparent Past, spiritual inheritance (good or evil), actual grandparent

Grapes Fruit of the vine, cup of the Lord

Grass Frailty of the flesh

Grasshopper Destruction

Green Prosperity, growth, life

Hammer Word of God

Hand Symbol of strength, power, action, possession

Harp Praise, worship to God

Head Authority, thoughts, mind

Heart Emotions, motivations, desires

Helmet Protection for thoughts, mind

Hen One who gathers, protects

Hills Elevation, high, loftiness

Horn Power, strength, defense

Horse Power, strength, conquest

House Home, dwelling place, the Church

Incense Prayer, intercessions, and worship

Jewels People of God

Key Authority, power to bind or loose, lock or unlock

Kiss Agreement, covenant, enticement, betrayal, covenant breaker, deception, seduction, friend

Knee Reverence, humility

Ladder Christ connecting Heaven and earth

Lamb Humility, the Church, Christ

Lead Weight, wickedness, sin, burden, judgment, fool, foolishness

Leaf Life amidst propserity

Legs Man's walk, man's strength

Leopard Swiftness, usually associated with vengeance

Lilies Beauty, majesty

Lion Royalty and kingship bravery, confidence

Lips Witness

Mechanic Minister, Christ, prophet, pastor, counselor

Mice Devourer, curse, plague, timid

Milk Foundational truth, nourishment

Mirror God's Word or one's heart, looking at oneself, looking back, memory, past, vanity

Miscarriage Abort, failure, loss, repentance, unjust judgment

Money Power, provision, wealth, natural talents and skills, spiritual riches, power, authority, trust in human strength, covetousness

Monkey Foolishness, clinging, mischief, dishonesty, addiction

Moon Symbol of light in darkness, sign of the Son of Man

Moth Symbol of destruction

Mother Source, Church, love, kindness, spiritual or natural mother

Mother-in-Law Legalism, meddler, trouble, natural mother-in-law

Mountain Kingdoms, dignity, permanence

Mouth Witness, good or evil

Nail Security, establish

Neck Force, loveliness, or inflexibility, meekness, rebellion

Nest Home, place to dwell

Net Symbol of a catcher as in the parables, catching men

Nine Judgment, finality

Nineteen Barren, ashamed, repentant, selflessness, without self-righteousness; faith

Nose Breath, discernment

Nudity Uncovered or flesh, self-justification, self-righteousness, impure, ashamed, stubborn, temptation, lust, sexual control, exhibitionism, truth, honest, nature

Oil Holy Spirit, anointing

One God as a unity and as a source, new beginnings

One Hundred Fullness, full measure, full recompense, full reward; God's election of grace, children of promise

One Hundred Fifty-Three Revival, ingathering, final harvest of souls

One Hundred Forty-Four God's ultimate in creation

One Hundred Nineteen The resurrection day; Lord's day

One Hundred Twenty End of all flesh, beginning of life in the Spirit; divine period of probation

One Thousand Maturity, full stature, mature service, mature judgment; divine completeness and the glory of God

Orange Danger, great jeopardy, harm; a common color combination is orange and black, which usually signifies great evil or danger; bright or fire orange can be power, force, energy

Oven Testing or judgment

Palace Heaven, royalty

Palm Tree Victory, worship

Pasture Places of spiritual nourishment

Pearl Spiritual truth

Pen/Pencil Tongue, indelible words, covenant, agreement, contract, vow, publish, record, permanent, unforgettable, gossip

Pig Ignorance, hypocrisy, religious unbelievers, unclean people, selfish, gluttonous, vicious, vengeful

Pillar Strength, steadfastness, assistance

Pink Flesh, sensual, immoral, moral (as in a heart of flesh); chaste, a female infant

Pit Prison, oppression

Plumbline Standards of God, measuring of a life

Plow Breaking new ground

Pregnancy In process, sin or righteousness in process, desire, anticipation, expectancy

Pumpkin Witchcraft, deception, snare, witch, trick

Purple Royalty, wealth, prosperity

Rabbit Increase, fast growth, multiplication; hare can be satan and his evil spirits

Raccoon Mischief, night raider, rascal, thief, bandit, deceitful

Rain Blessing, God's Word, revival

Rainbow Covenant

Ram Sacrifice

Raven Evil, satan

Red Suffering, sacrifice, or sin

Rings Eternity, completion

River Revival, refreshing

Roach Infestation, unclean spirits, hidden sin

Robe Covering, royalty

Rock Christ our rock, stability

Rod Rule, correction, guidance

Roof Covering, oversight

Root Spiritual source, offspring

Rope Binding, bondage

Rose Christ and His Church

Rubies Value, worth, significance

Salt Incorruptibility, preserve from corruption, covenant

Sand Similar to seed, generations

Sapphire Beauty, value

Scorpion Evil spirits, evil men; pinch of pain

Sea Wicked nations

Serpent satan and evil spirits

Seven Completeness, perfection

Seventeen Spiritual order, incomplete, immature, undeveloped, childish, victory

Seventy Number of increase, perfected ministry

Sheep Chant, the people of God, innocent

Shield Sign of protection

Shoe Sign of walking, protection for your walk

Shoulder Bearing the burden of another, authority, rulership

Sister Spiritual sister, Church, self, natural sister

Six Hundred Warfare

Six-Six-Six Sign of the mark of the beast, antichrist

Sixteen Free-spirited, without boundaries, without law, without sin, salvation; love

Sixty Pride

Sixty-Six Idol worship

Skins Covering

Smoke Blinding power

Snow Spotlessness, radiance

Sparrow Small value but precious

Spring New beginning, revival, fresh start, renewal, regeneration, salvation, refreshing

Stars Israel, generations

Steps Signs of spiritual progress

Stone Might, permanence

Storms Misfortune, difficulty, trials

Summer Harvest, opportunity, trial, heat of affliction

Sun Glory, brightness, light, Christ

Sword Scriptures, Christ

Teeth Consuming power

Ten Law and order

Tent A temporary covering, not a permanent home

Thirteen Sign of rebellion, backsliding, apostasy

Thirty Maturity for ministry

Thirty-Eight Slavery

Thirty-Five Hope

Thirty-Four Naming of a son

Thirty-Nine Disease

Thirty-Seven The Word of God

Thirty-Six Enemy

Thirty-Three Promise

Thirty-Two Covenant

Three Hundred Faithful remnant (Gideon's army)

Tiger Danger, powerful minister (both good and evil)

Tin Dross, waste, worthless, cheap, purification

Tongue Language, speech

Train Continuous, unceasing work, connected, fast, Church

Trap Snare, danger, trick

Trees Nations, individuals, the Church

Tunnel Passage, transition, way of escape, troubling experience, trial, hope

Twelve Divine government, apostolic government

Twenty-Eight Eternal life

Twenty-Five The forgiveness of sins

Twenty-Four Symbol of Priesthood courses and order

Twenty-Nine Departure

Twenty-One Exceeding sinfulness, of sin

Twenty-Seven Preaching of the Gospel

Twenty-Six The Gospel of Christ

Twenty-Three Death

Twenty-Two Light

Two Sign for witness, testimony, or unity

Two Hundred Insufficiency

Van Family (natural or Church), family ministry, fellowship

Vine Symbol for Israel, Christ and His Church

Vulture Sign of uncleanness and devourer

Wall Fortification, division, refuge

Watch Prophetic, intercession, being on guard

Waters Nations of earth, agitation, undercurrents, crosscurrents

Well Places of refreshment, source of water of life

Wheel Transport, a circle, speed, spiritual activity

Whirlwind Hurricane, sweeping power, unable to resist

Wind Breath of life, power of God

Window Blessings of Heaven, openness

Wine Holy Spirit

Wine-Skin Spiritual structure

Wings Protection, spiritual transport

Winter Barren, death, dormant, waiting, cold, unfriendly

Wolf satan and evil, false ministries, and teachers

Woman Church, virgin or harlot

Wood Humanity

Wrestling Striving, deliverance, resistance, persistence, trial, tribulation, spirit attempting to gain control

Yellow Gift, marriage, family, honor, deceitful gift, timidity, fear, cowardliness

Yoke Servitude, slavery, or fellowship

Directions

East Beginning: law (therefore blessed or cursed); birth; first (see Gen. 11:2; Job 38:24).

Front Future or Now: as in front yard; in the presence of; prophecy; immediate; current (see Gen 6:11; Rev 1:19).

North Spiritual: judgment; Heaven; spiritual warfare (as in "taking your inheritance"). See Proverbs 25:23; Jeremiah 1:13-14.

Left Spiritual: weakness (of man) and therefore God's strength or ability; rejected. (Left Turn = spiritual change). See Judges 3:20-21; Second Corinthians 12:9-10.

South Natural: sin; world; temptation; trial; flesh; corruption; deception (see Josh.10:40; Job 37:9).

Right Natural: authority; power; the strength of man (flesh) or the power of God revealed through man; accepted. (Right Turn = natural change). See Matthew 5:29a,30a; First Peter 3:22.

West End: grace; death; last; conformed (see Exod. 10:19; Luke 12:54).

Back Past: as in backyard or back door; previous event or experience (good or evil); that which is behind (in time—for example, past sins or the sins of forefathers); unaware; unsuspecting; hidden; memory (see Gen. 22:13; Josh. 8:4).

People/Relatives/Trades

Baby New: beginning; work; idea; the Church; sin; innocent; dependant; helpless; natural baby (see 1 Cor. 3:1; Isa. 43:19).

Carpenter Builder: preacher; evangelist; laborer (good or evil); Christ (see 2 Kings 22:6; Isa. 41:7).

Doctor Healer: Christ; preacher; authority; medical doctor, when naturally interpreted (see Mark 2:17; 2 Chron. 16:12).

Drunk Influenced: under a spell (i.e., under the influence of the Holy Spirit or a demon spirit); controlled; fool; stubborn; rebellious; witchcraft (see Eph. 5:18; Prov. 14:16).

Employer Servants: pastor, Christ; satan; actual employer, when naturally interpreted (see Col. 3:22; 2 Pet. 2:19).

Giant Strongman: stronghold, challenge; obstacle; trouble (see Num. 13:32-33).

Indian First: flesh (as in "the old man"); firstborn; chief; fierce; savvy; native (see Col. 3:9; Gen. 49:3).

Police Authority: natural (civil) or spiritual authority (pastors, etc.), good or evil; protection; angels or demons; an enforcer of a curse of the Law (see Rom. 13:1; Luke 12:11).

Vehicles and Parts

Airplane Person or Work: the Church; ministry; oversight (soaring = moved by the Spirit). See Habakkuk 1:8; Judges 13:25.

Automobile Life: person; ministry (new car = new ministry or new way of life). See Genesis 41:43; Second Kings 10:16.

Auto Wreck Strife: contention; conflict, calamity; mistake, or sin in ministry (as in "failure to maintain right-of-way"). See Nahum 2:4.

Bicycle Works: works of the flesh (not of faith); self-righteousness; messenger (see Gal. 5:4,19).

Boat Church or Personal Ministry: (sailboat = moved by the Spirit; powerboat = powerful or fast progress). See Genesis 6:16; First Timothy 1:19.

Brakes Stop: hindrance; resist; wait (see Acts 16:6-7; 2 Pet. 2:14).

Helicoptor Ministry: personal; individual; the Church; versatile; stationary (when unmoving). See Second Timothy 4:2; Romans 8:14.

Jet Ministry or Minister: powerful; fast (passenger jet = Church; fighter = individual person). See Genesis 41:43; Second Kings 10:16.

Motorcycle Individual: personal ministry; independent; rebellion; selfish; pride; swift progress (see 2 Pet. 2:10; 1 Sam. 15:23).

Pickup Truck Work: personal ministry or natural work (see 1 Chron. 13:7; Gal. 6:5).

Rearview Mirror Word: (driving backward using the rearview mirror = operating by the letter of the Word instead of by God's Spirit); legalistic; looking back (see Luke 9:62; 2 Cor. 3:6; Gen. 19:26).

Raft Adrift: without direction; aimless; powerless (see Eph. 4:14).

Tractor Powerful Work: slow but powerful ministry (see Acts 1:8; 4:33).

Tractor-Trailer Large Burden: ministry; powerful and/or large work (truck size is often in proportion to the burden or size of the work).

Miscellaneous

Ankles Faith: weak ankles = weak faith; unsupported; undependable (see Ezek. 47:3).

Arm Strength or Weakness: Savior; deliverer; helper; aid; reaching out (see Isa. 52:10; Ps. 136:12).

Bank Secure: Church; dependable; safe; saved; sure (as in "you can bank on it"); reserved in Heaven (see Luke 19:23; Matt. 6:20).

Binoculars Insight: understanding; prophetic vision; future event (see John 16:13; 2 Cor. 3:13, 16).

Bleeding Wounded: hurt, naturally or emotionally; dying spiritually; offended; gossip; unclean (see Ps. 147:3; Prov. 18:8).

Blood Transfusion Change: regeneration; salvation; deliverance (see Titus 3:5; Rom. 12:2).

Bridge Faith: trial; way; joined (see Gen. 32:22; 1 Cor. 10:13).

Butter Works: doing (or not doing) the Word or will of God; deceptive motives, works, or words; smooth (see Ps. 55:21; Prov. 30:33).

Calendar Time: date; event; appointment (see Hos. 6:11).

Cards Facts: honesty (as in "putting all your cards on the table"); truth; expose or reveal; dishonest; cheat; deceitful (see Rom. 12:17).

Carnival Worldly: exhibitionism; divination; competition (see Acts 16:16; Luke 21:34).

Chair Position: seat of authority; rest (see Esther 3:1; Rev.13:2).

Check Faith: the currency of the Kingdom of God; provision; trust (see Heb. 11:1; Mark 4:40).

Choking Hinder: stumbling over something (as in "that's too much to swallow"); hatred or anger (as in "I could choke him!"). See Mark 4:19.

Christmas Gift: season of rejoicing; spiritual gifts; a surprise; good will (see Luke 11:13; 1 Cor. 14:1).

Closet Private: personal, prayer; secret sin; hidden (see Matt. 6:6; Luke 8:17).

Coffee Bitter or Stimulant: repentance; reaping what one has sown; desire for revenge (bitter envying). See Numbers 9:11; Job 13:26.

Ditch Habit: religious tradition; addition; lust; passion (see Matt. 15:14; Ps. 7:15).

Dominoes Continuous: chain reaction (see Lev. 26:37).

Earthquake Upheaval: change (by crisis), repentance; trial; God's judgment; disaster; trauma (see Acts 16:26; Isa. 29:6).

Echo Repetition: gossip; accusation; voice of many; mocking (see Luke 23:21).

Egg Idea: new thought; plan; promise; potential (see Luke 11:12; 1 Tim. 4:15).

Fence Barrier: boundaries; obstacles; religious traditions; doctrines; inhibitions (see Gen. 11:6; Jer. 15:20).

Garbage (Dump) Rejected: hell; evil; vile; corruption (see Mark 9:47-48; 1 Cor. 9:27).

Gasoline Fuel: prayer, inflammatory; gossip; contention; danger (see Jude 20; Prov. 26:20-21).

Gloves Covering: protection; save; careful (as in "handle with kid gloves"). See Psalms 24:3-4; First Timothy 4:14-15.

Grass, Mowed Chastisement: sickness; financial need or distress; emotional and mental depression or anguish (see Amos 7:1-2; 1 Cor. 11:30-32).

Graveyard Hidden: past; curse; evil inheritance; hypocrisy; demon (see Matt. 23:27; Luke 11:44).

Gravel Pit Source: the Word of God; abundant supply (see Deut. 8:9; 2 Tim. 2:15).

Ironing Correction: change; sanctification; exhorting; teaching righteousness; God's discipline; pressure (from trials). See Ephesians 5:27.

Ladder Ascend or Descend: escape; enable; way; steps (see Gen. 28:12-13; John 3:13).

Lips Words: seduction; speech (see Prov. 7:21; 10:19).

Map Directions: Word of God; correction; advice (see Prov. 6:23).

Microphone Voice: authority; ministry; influence (see Matt. 10:27).

Mirror Word or One's Heart: God's Word; looking back; memory, past; vanity; Moses's Law (see 1 Cor. 13:12; Prov. 27:19).

Muddy Road Flesh: man's way; lust; passion; temptation; difficulty caused by the weakness of the flesh (see Ps. 69:2; Isa. 57:20).

Newspaper Announcement: important event; public exposure; news; gossip (see Luke 8:17).

Oven Heart: heat of passion; imagination; meditation; judgment (see Hos. 7:6; Ps. 21:9).

Paint Brush Covering: house painter's brush: regeneration; remodel; renovate; love; artist's paint brush; words; illustrative; eloquent; humorous; articulate (see 1 Pet. 4:8; Titus 3:5).

Parachuting Leave: bail out; escape; flee; saved (see 2 Cor. 6:17; Jer. 50:28).

Perfume Seduction: enticement; temptation; persuasion; deception (see Prov. 7:7,10,13; Eccles. 10:1).

Pie Whole: business endeavors; part of the action (see Luke 12:13).

Play Worship: idolatry; covetousness; true worship; spiritual warfare; strife; competition (see Col. 3:5; 1 Cor. 9:24).

Postage Stamp Seal: authority; authorization; small or seemingly insignificant, but powerful (see Esther 8:8; John 6:27).

Pot/Pan/Bowl Vessel: doctrine; traditions; a determination or resolve; form of the truth; a person (see Rom. 2:20; Jer. 1:13).

Radio Unchangeable: unbelief; unrelenting; contentious; unceasing; tradition (see Prov. 27:15).

Railroad Track Tradition: unchanging; habit; stubborn; Gospel (see Mark 7:9, 13; Col. 2:8).

Rape Violation: abuse of authority; hate; desire for revenge; murder (see 2 Sam. 13:12, 14-15; Deut. 22:25-26).

Refrigerator Heart: motive; attitude; stored in heart; harbor (see Matt. 12:35; Mark 7:21-22).

Rocking Chair Old: past, memories; meditation; retirement; rest (see Jer. 6:16).

Roller Coaster Unstable: emotional instability; unfaithfulness; wavering; manic-depressive; depression; trials; excitement (see Isa. 40:4; James 1:6-8).

Roller Skates Speed: fast; swift advancement or progress (see Rom. 9:28).

Round Spiritual: (a round face, ring, building, etc.); grace; mercy; compassion; forgiveness (see Lev. 19:27).

Sea Coast Boundary: flesh (which contains and limits the spirit of man); limitations; weights (see Jer. 5:22; 47:6-7).

Shovel Tongue: prayer; confession; slander; dig; search; inquire (see 2 Kings 3:16-17; Deut. 23:13).

Skiing Faith: (water or snowskiing); supported by God's power through faith; fast progress (see John 6:19, 21; Matt. 14:29-31).

Sleep Unconscious: unaware; hidden or covered; ignorance; danger; death (see Isa. 29:10; Rom. 13:11).

Smile Friendly: kindness; benevolent; without offense; seduction (see Prov. 18:24).

Square Legalistic: (square eyeglasses, buildings, etc.); religious or religion; no mercy; hard or harsh; of the world (see Lev. 19:9).

Sweeping Cleaning: repentance; change; removing obstacles (see 2 Cor. 7:1,11).

Swimming Spiritual: serving God; worship; operating in the gifts of the Spirit; prophecy (see Ezek. 47:5; Eph. 3:8).

Teeth, False Replacement: wisdom or knowledge gained through experience or previous failures; logical reasoning; tradition (see Rom. 5:3-4; Col. 2:8).

Toothache Trial: unfaithful; no faith; unbelief. (Tooth = wisdom; ache = suffering; broken = potential pain, i.e., when pressure is applied.) See Proverbs 25:19.

Television Vision: message; prophecy; preaching; news; evil influence; wickedness (see Num. 24:16; Dan. 2:19).

Thunder Change or Without Understanding: (of what the Spirit is saying or of the signs of the times); dispensational change (i.e., a change in the way God deals with His people); warning of impending judgment or trouble (see John 12:28-29; Ps. 18:13).

Title/Deed Ownership: authorization; possession (see Gen. 23:20).

Tree Stump Unbelief: roots; tenacious; obstacle; immovable; hope (see Job 14:7-9).

Urinating Spirit: full bladder = pressure. Compelling urge; temptation (such as sexual lust or strife); bladder infection or cancer = offense; enmity (see Prov. 17:14).

Washcloth Truth: doctrine; understanding (dirty cloth = false doctrine: insincere apology; error). See Psalms 51:7; Job 14:4.

Watermelon Fruit: the fruit of good or evil works; the pleasures of sin (Seeds = Words; Water = Spirit; Sweetness = Strength; Green = Life; Red = Passion; Yellow = Gifts). See Numbers 11:5; Proverbs 1:31.

Western Frontier: ("the wild west," a western movie, etc.); pioneer; spiritual warfare; boldness; challenge (see Deut. 20:10; Josh. 3:4).

Additional Resources by James W. & Michal Ann Goll

Prophetic Encounters

Featuring James W. Goll
Music by John Belt

Be prepared to receive a Prophetic Encounter as James W. Goll shares stories, and personal experiences, reads scripture and releases prayers of impartation. Titles include: Beautiful, Bread of His Presence, Rock the Nations, Over Here, Dread Champions, Giants of Faith, Days of Acceleration, The Golden Anointing, and many more...

$15.00

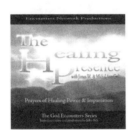

The Healing Presence

Featuring James W. & Michal Ann Goll
Music by John Belt

Receive God's Healing Presence as James W. & Michal Ann Goll read scripture, share stories, and release prayers of impartation. "The Lord really visited us in this recording!"
Titles include: The Hem of His Garment, The Day of Healing, How Lovely, The Healing River, and many more...

$15.00

Invitation To Intimacy

This CD was professionally recorded at the Wagner Leadership Institute as James W. Goll was caught up into another realm. It contains over 60 minutes of prophetic, spontaneous worship and teaching with keyboard and instrumentation with John Belt. Soak with this one!

$15.00

Sacred Fire

by John Belt

This non-stop instrumental CD will take you on a journey with many creative sounds. The sacred fire is fire that burns in our lives before God in prayer. Songs include Waters of Moriah, Sacred Fire, Celestial Door, Heaven's Shores and others . . .

$15.00

For Additional Products by James W. and Michal Ann Goll

Visit www.jamesgoll.com | Call 1~877~200~1604

Study Guides by James W. Goll

Over the years, James W. Goll has taught these practical tools to help people all over the world learn a prophetic lifestyle. The comprehensive study guides in this series can be used either for individual study or with a class or small group. Following each detailed lesson are simple questions for reflection. As you work through these lessons, you will be inspired to take your place in God's prophetic army.

Equipping in the Prophetic / Enlisting a Prophetic Army

Prophetic Foundations

The first of this series on the prophetic. These 12 lessons include:
For the Many - Not the Few, The History of the Prophetic,
Intimacy in the Prophetic, Power & Perils of the Prophetic Spirit
Seven Expressions of the Prophetic Spirit, Prophesy Life,
The Prophetic Song of the Lord, and more...

$15.00

Experiencing Dreams & Visions

This is the second Guide in the series. These 12 lessons include:
God's Multi-faceted Voice, Visionary Revelation, Journaling,
Tools For Interpreting Revelation, Dream Language,
Receiving and Judging Revelation, Wisdom in Handling Revelation,
Dream Language I & II, Tips for Interpratations , and more...

$15.00

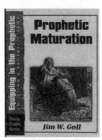

Prophetic Maturation

This is the third Guide in the series. These 12 lessons Include:
Called Into Character, From Character to Commissioning,
Seizing your Prophetic Destiny Parts 1 & 2, The Cross -
The Prophetic Lifestyle, Four levels of Prophetic Ministry,
The Seer and the Prophet: Similarities and Differences, and more...

$15.00

Understanding Supernatural Encounters

This is the fourth Guide in the series. These 12 lessons Include:
Keys to the Supernatural, How to Receive Revelation,
Demonstrating Three Models, The Deception of the Anointing,
Levels Of Supernatural Visions Parts 1 & 2, Trances Defined,
Ministry and Function of Angels, Current Day Accounts of Angelic
Activity, and more...

$15.00

www.jamesgoll.com or Call 1~877~200~1604